161/400

THE VISUAL DICTIONARY *of*
SHIPS *and*
SAILING

Thimble

Seizing

Crown

Sheave

Strop

Tail

A STROPPED BLOCK

ONE-MAN DIVING SUIT

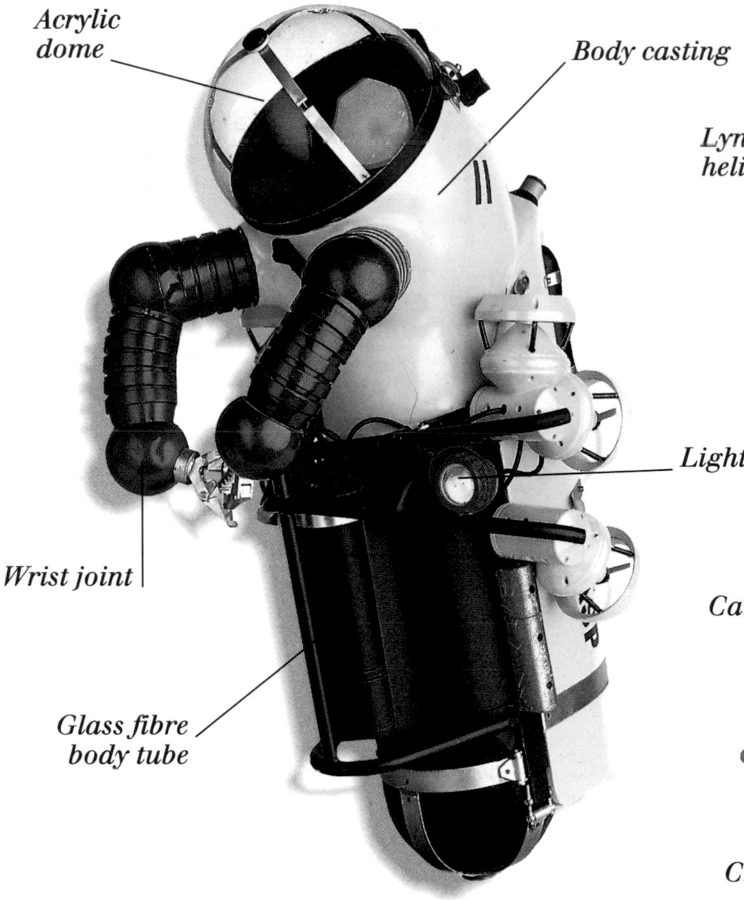

Acrylic dome

Body casting

Light

Wrist joint

Glass fibre body tube

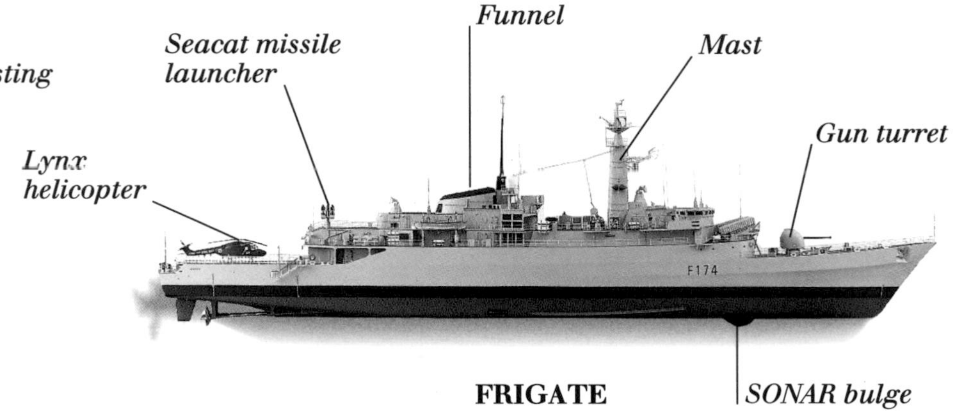

FRIGATE

Seacat missile launcher

Lynx helicopter

Funnel

Mast

Gun turret

F174

SONAR bulge

BOW OF A 74-GUN SHIP

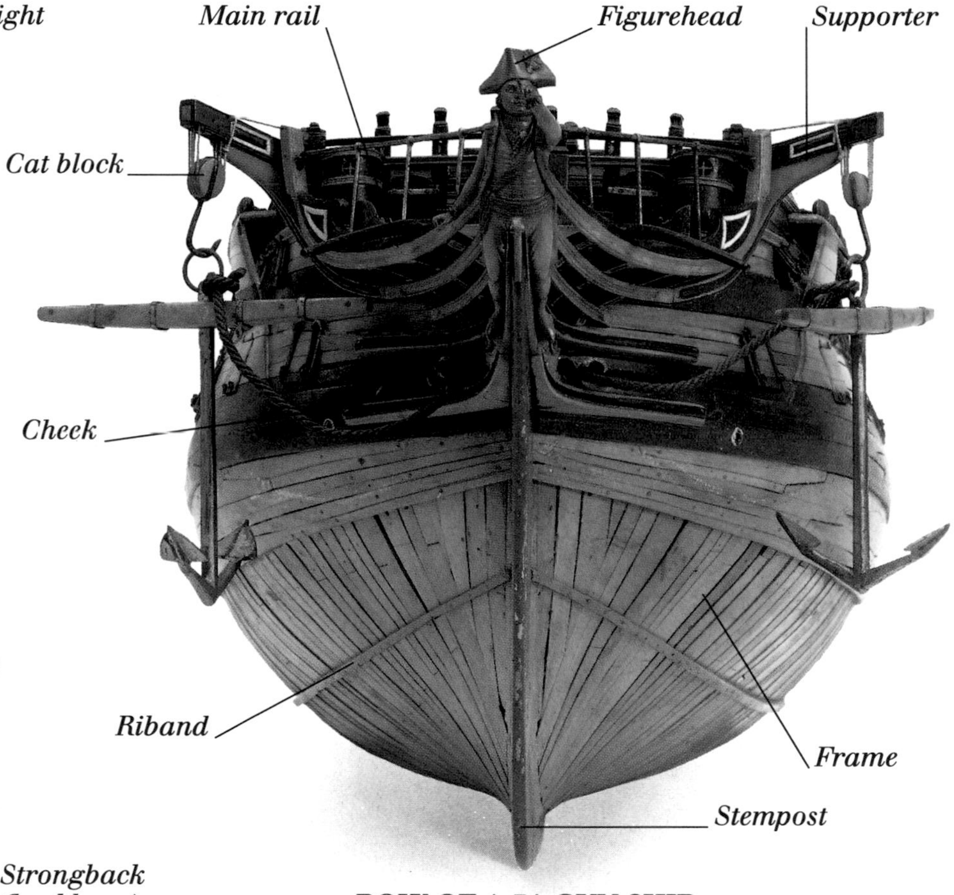

Main rail

Figurehead

Supporter

Cat block

Cheek

Riband

Frame

Stempost

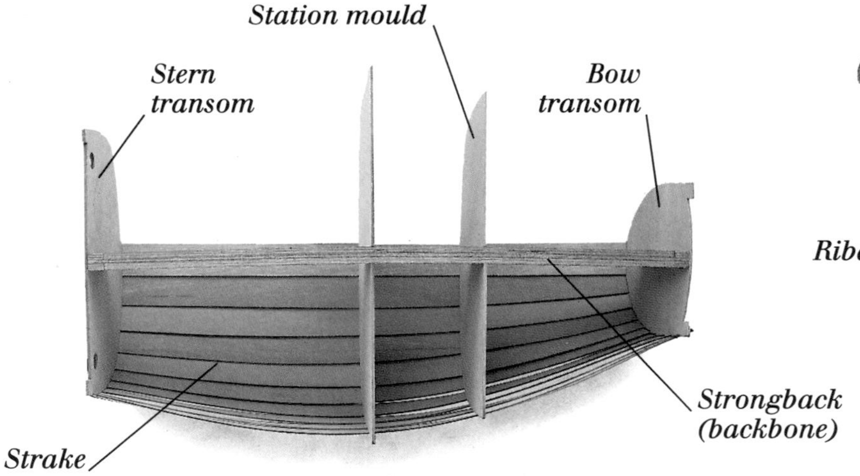

DINGHY JIG WITH PLANKING

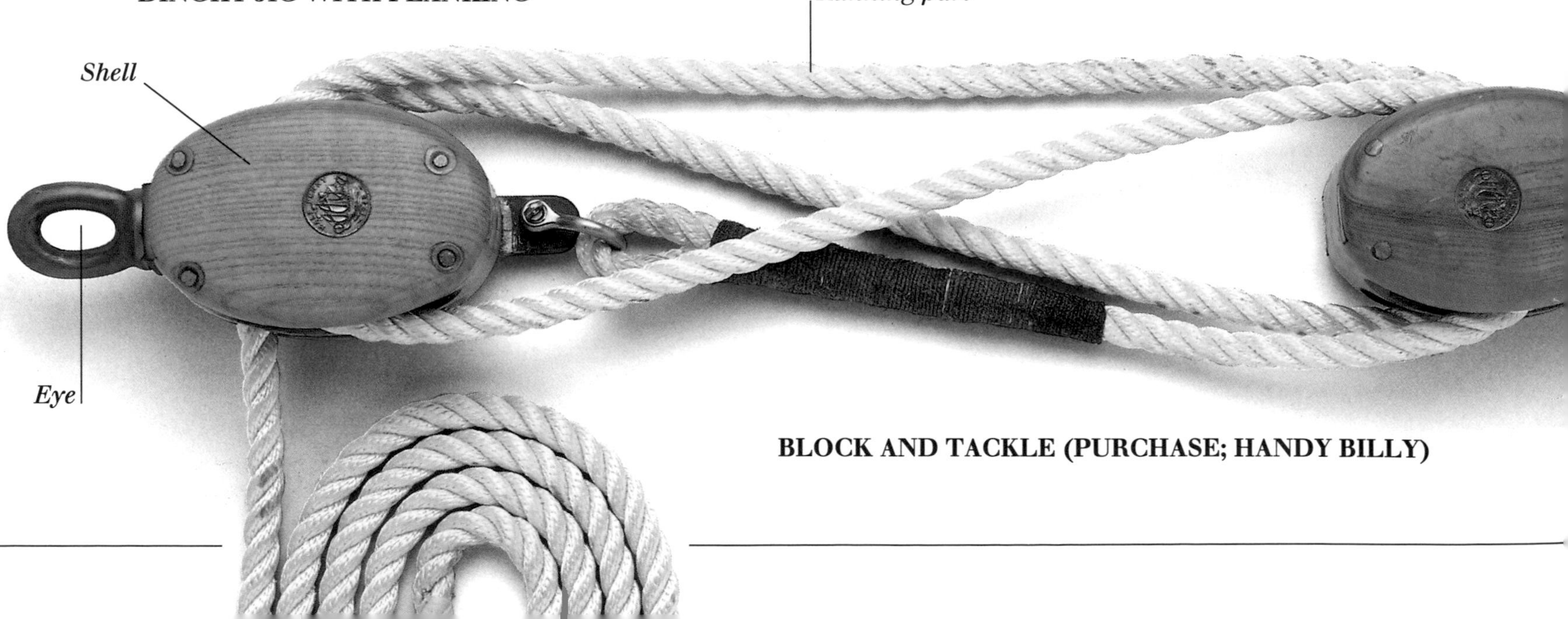

Station mould

Stern transom

Bow transom

Strongback (backbone)

Strake

BLOCK AND TACKLE (PURCHASE; HANDY BILLY)

Running part

Shell

Eye

EYEWITNESS VISUAL DICTIONARIES

THE VISUAL
DICTIONARY *of*
SHIPS *and*
SAILING

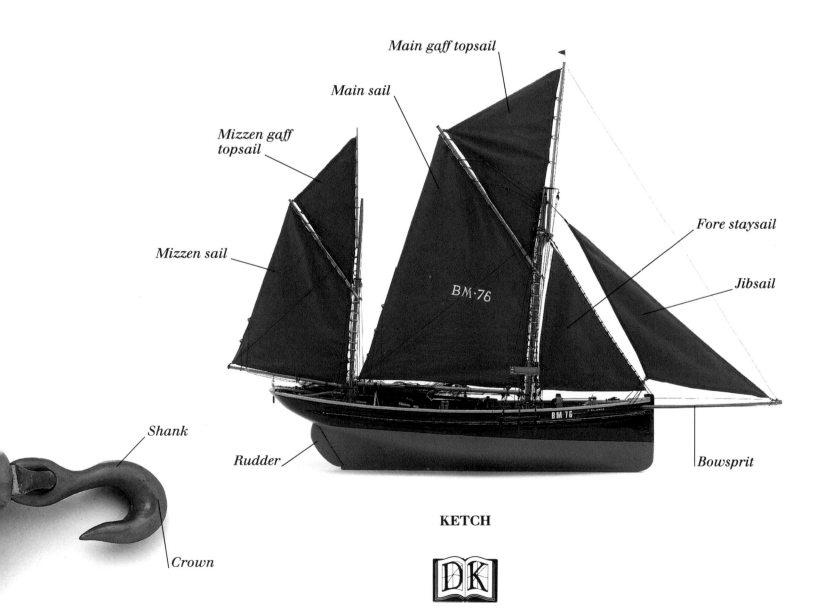

Main gaff topsail

Main sail

Mizzen gaff topsail

Fore staysail

Mizzen sail

Jibsail

BM·76

Shank

Rudder

Bowsprit

Crown

KETCH

DK

DORLING KINDERSLEY

LONDON · NEW YORK · STUTTGART

A DORLING KINDERSLEY BOOK

PROJECT ART EDITOR STEPHEN KNOWLDEN
DESIGN ASSISTANT PAUL CALVER

PROJECT EDITOR ROGER TRITTON

SERIES ART EDITOR PAUL WILKINSON
ART DIRECTOR CHEZ PICTHALL
MANAGING EDITOR RUTH MIDGLEY

PHOTOGRAPHY JAMES STEVENSON, DAVE KING, STEVE GORTON, TIM RIDLEY

PRODUCTION HILARY STEPHENS

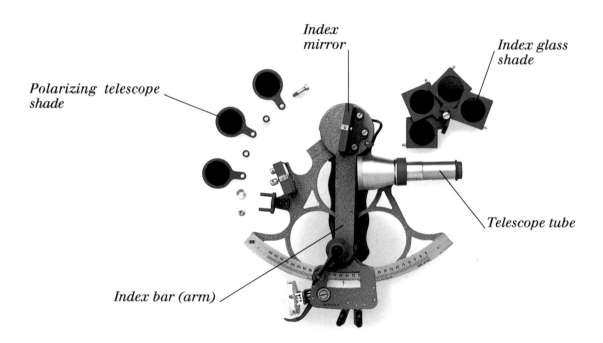

Index mirror

Index glass shade

Polarizing telescope shade

Telescope tube

Index bar (arm)

MODERN SEXTANT

FIRST PUBLISHED IN GREAT BRITAIN IN 1991
BY DORLING KINDERSLEY LIMITED,
9 HENRIETTA STREET, LONDON WC2E 8PS

A CIP CATALOGUE RECORD FOR THIS BOOK IS AVAILABLE FROM THE BRITISH LIBRARY

ISBN 0-86318-702-1

REPRODUCED BY GRB GRAFICA, VERONA, ITALY
PRINTED AND BOUND BY ARNOLDO MONDADORI, VERONA, ITALY

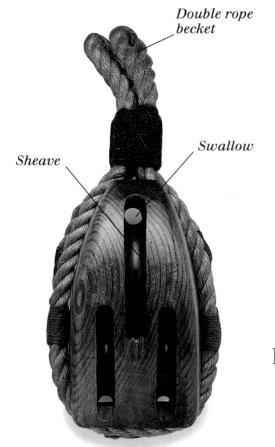

Double rope becket

Sheave

Swallow

DUTCH TRIPLE FIDDLE BLOCK

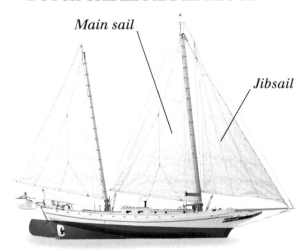

Main sail

Jibsail

CHESAPEAKE BAY BATEAU

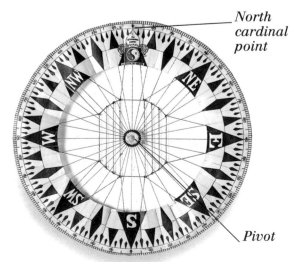

North cardinal point

Pivot

KELVIN LIGHT DRY COMPASS CARD

Contents

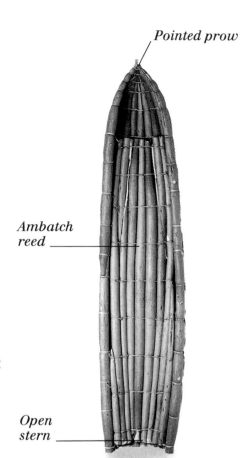

Pointed prow

Ambatch reed

Open stern

REED BOAT OF KENYA

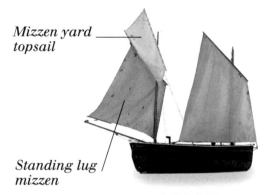

Mizzen yard topsail

Standing lug mizzen

LUGGER

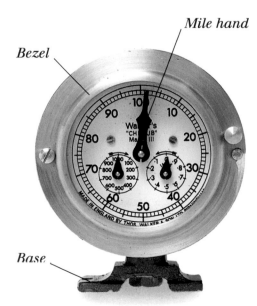

Mile hand

Bezel

Base

PATENT LOG REGISTER

The first boats

EARLY PEOPLE NEEDED BOATS TO CROSS WATER, to travel, to trade and hunt, and to fish. They propelled their boats by hand, paddle, punting pole, or simple sail. Other than a floating tree trunk, man's first means of water transport was probably a raft. The Australian raft (right) could be built with the most elementary tools. Dugout logs and reeds – which are very light – were the materials most often used for early boats. The reed-built caballito was paddled through the surf of South American coastal waters, more like a float than a boat. The circular Iraqi guffa was used to carry cargo. It was simple to construct, and was often discarded once the journey was over. The guffa was made waterproof by being covered with pitch. By the third millenium B.C. the Egyptians were constructing sickle-shaped boats, like that at the bottom of the page, with cedar from Lebanon. The Egyptians also harnessed the wind with simple sails like that on the contemporary model of a travelling boat opposite. These boats were sailed from the Nile to trade with countries around the Mediterranean Sea.

WESTERN AUSTRALIAN RAFT

Wooden peg

Flat end

Shaped log

Pointed prow

Scarfed joint

Dugout section

Built-up side

Ambatch reed

Tie

Open stern

Square stern

HAITIAN DUGOUT CANOE

REED BOAT OF KENYA

Pomegranate stick

Twine

Straw

Pitch covering

IRAQI GUFFA

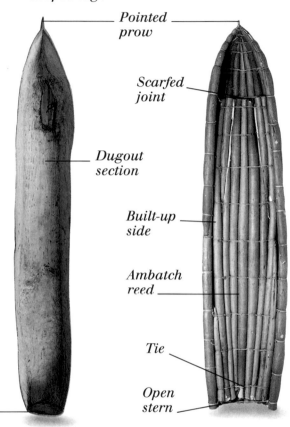

PERUVIAN CABALLITO (COASTAL REED BOAT)

Surf-riding prow

Cockpit

Bamboo reed

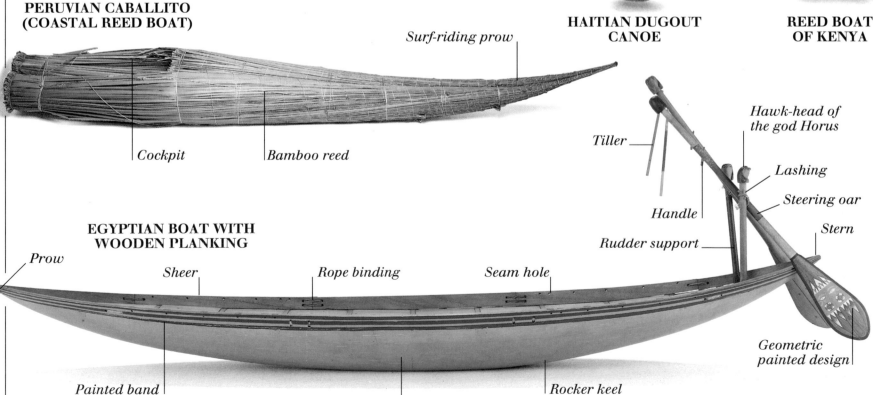

Hawk-head of the god Horus

Tiller

Lashing

Steering oar

Handle

Stern

Rudder support

EGYPTIAN BOAT WITH WOODEN PLANKING

Prow

Sheer

Rope binding

Seam hole

Painted band

Sickle-shaped wooden hull

Rocker keel

Geometric painted design

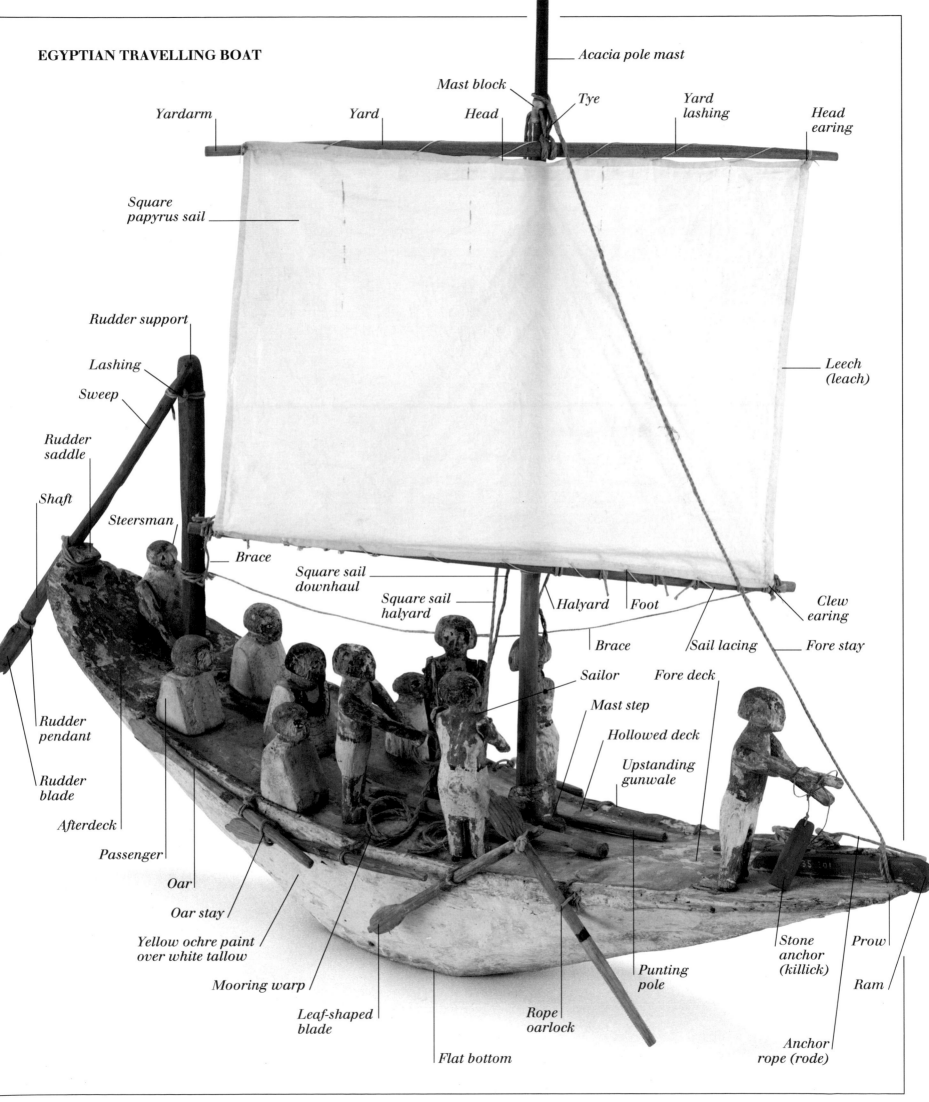

EGYPTIAN TRAVELLING BOAT

Acacia pole mast

Mast block

Tye

Yard lashing

Head earing

Yardarm

Yard

Head

Square papyrus sail

Leech (leach)

Rudder support

Lashing

Sweep

Rudder saddle

Shaft

Steersman

Brace

Square sail downhaul

Square sail halyard

Halyard

Foot

Clew earing

Brace

Sail lacing

Fore stay

Sailor

Fore deck

Mast step

Hollowed deck

Upstanding gunwale

Rudder pendant

Rudder blade

Afterdeck

Passenger

Oar

Oar stay

Yellow ochre paint over white tallow

Mooring warp

Leaf-shaped blade

Rope oarlock

Flat bottom

Punting pole

Stone anchor (killick)

Prow

Ram

Anchor rope (rode)

Ships of Greece and Rome

ROMAN ANCHOR

Stock

Shank

Palm

Acutely angled arm

Ring

Crown

IN THE EXPANSIVE EMPIRES OF GREECE AND ROME, powerful fleets were needed for battle, trade, and communication. Greek galleys were powered by a sail and many oars. A new armament, the embolos (ram), was fitted on to the galley bow. As ramming duels required fast and manoeuvrable boats, extra rows of oarsmen were added, culminating in the trireme. During the fifth and fourth centuries B.C., the trireme dominated the Mediterranean. It was powered by 170 oarsmen, rowing with one oar each. The oarsmen were ranged on three levels, as the model opposite shows. The trireme also carried archers and soldiers for boarding. Galleys were pulled out of the water when not in use, and were kept in dockyard ship-sheds. The merchant ships of the Greeks and Romans were mighty vessels too. The full-bodied Roman corbita, for example, could hold up to 400 tons and carried a cargo of spices, gems, silk, and animals. The construction of these boats was based on a stout hull with planking secured by mortice and tenon. Some of these ships embarked on long voyages, sailing even as far as India. To make them easier to steer, corbitas set a fore sail called an "artemon". It flew from a forward-leaning mast that was a forerunner of the long bowsprits carried by the great clipper ships of the 19th century.

ATTIC VASE SHOWING A GALLEY

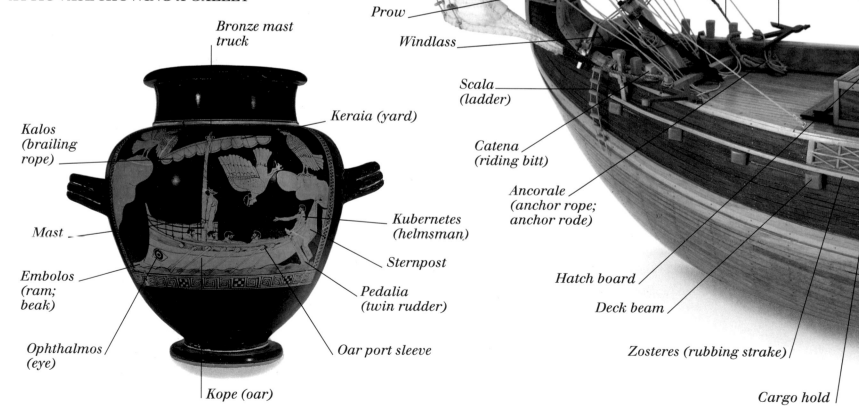

Bronze mast truck

Kalos (brailing rope)

Keraia (yard)

Mast

Embolos (ram; beak)

Kubernetes (helmsman)

Sternpost

Pedalia (twin rudder)

Ophthalmos (eye)

Oar port sleeve

Kope (oar)

ROMAN CORBITA

Double halyard

Bullseye

Antenna (yard)

Artemon (fore sail)

Oculus (eye)

Tabling

Bolt rope

Prow

Windlass

Scala (ladder)

Catena (riding bitt)

Ancorale (anchor rope; anchor rode)

Fore mast

Buntline

Brace

Roband (rope band)

Ceruchi (lift)

Heraldic device

Ring

Ruden (brail line)

Fore stay

Anchor

Sheet

Hatch board

Deck beam

Zosteres (rubbing strake)

Cargo hold

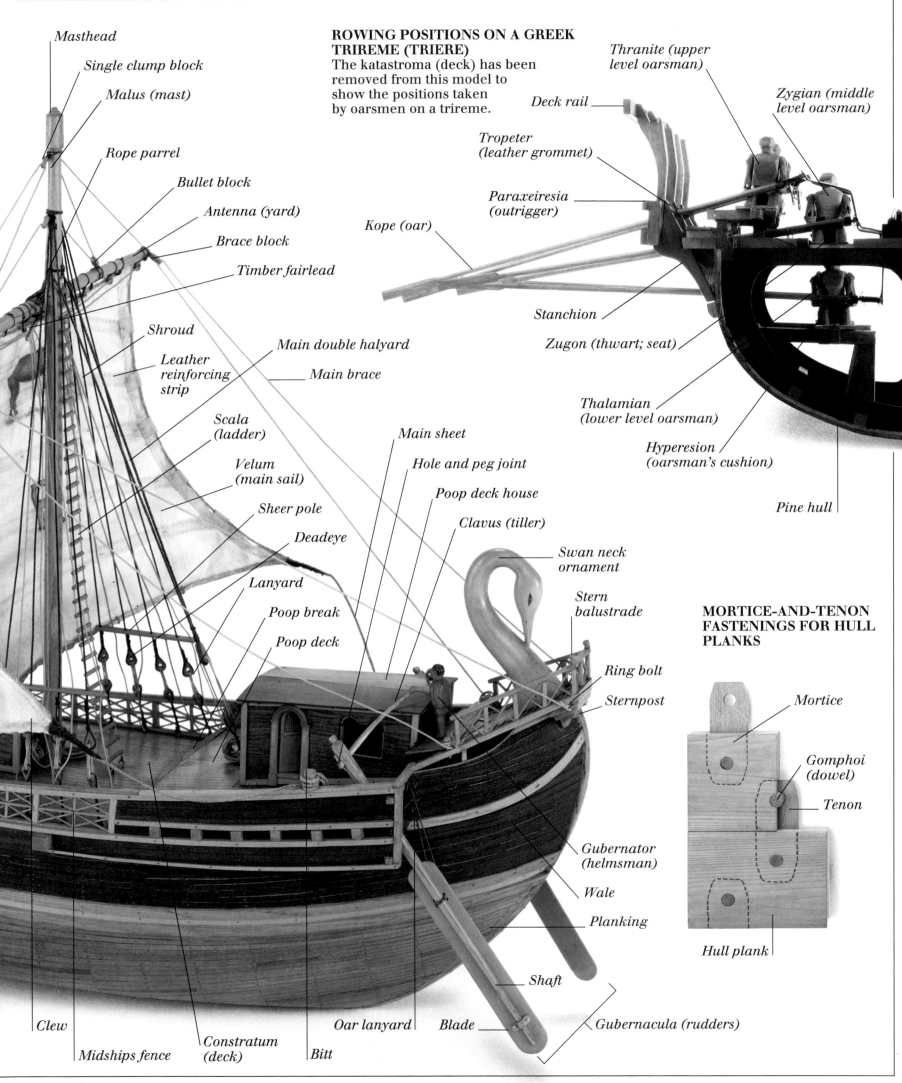

Masthead

Single clump block

Malus (mast)

Rope parrel

Bullet block

Antenna (yard)

Brace block

Timber fairlead

Shroud

Leather reinforcing strip

Main double halyard

Main brace

Scala (ladder)

Velum (main sail)

Sheer pole

Deadeye

Lanyard

Poop break

Poop deck

ROWING POSITIONS ON A GREEK TRIREME (TRIERE)
The katastroma (deck) has been removed from this model to show the positions taken by oarsmen on a trireme.

Deck rail

Tropeter (leather grommet)

Paraxeiresia (outrigger)

Kope (oar)

Main sheet

Hole and peg joint

Poop deck house

Clavus (tiller)

Swan neck ornament

Stern balustrade

Thranite (upper level oarsman)

Zygian (middle level oarsman)

Stanchion

Zugon (thwart; seat)

Thalamian (lower level oarsman)

Hyperesion (oarsman's cushion)

Pine hull

MORTICE-AND-TENON FASTENINGS FOR HULL PLANKS

Ring bolt

Sternpost

Gubernator (helmsman)

Wale

Planking

Mortice

Gomphoi (dowel)

Tenon

Hull plank

Clew

Midships fence

Constratum (deck)

Bitt

Oar lanyard

Blade

Shaft

Gubernacula (rudders)

9

Viking ships

In the dark ages and early medieval times, the longships of Scandinavia were one of the most feared sights for people of northern Europe. The Vikings launched raids from Scandinavia every summer in longships equipped with a single steering oar on the right, or "steerboard", side (hence "starboard"). A longship had one row of oars on each side and a single sail. The hull had clinker (overlapping) planks. Prowheads adorned fighting ships during campaigns of war. The sailing longship was also used for local coastal travel. The karv below was probably built as transport for an important family, while the smaller faering (top right) was a rowing boat only. The fleet of William of Normandy that invaded England in 1066 owed much to the Viking boatbuilding tradition, and has been depicted in the Bayeux Tapestry (above). Seals used by port towns and royal courts through the ages provide an excellent record of contemporary ship design. The seal opposite shows how ships changed from the Viking period to the end of the Middle Ages. The introduction of the fighting platform – the castle – and the addition of extra masts and sails changed the character of the medieval ship. Note also that the steering oar has been replaced by a centred rudder.

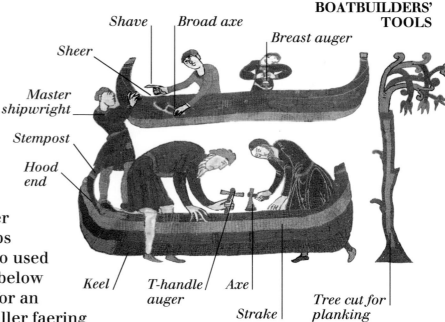

BOATBUILDERS' TOOLS

Shave
Broad axe
Breast auger
Sheer
Master shipwright
Stempost
Hood end
Keel
T-handle auger
Axe
Strake
Tree cut for planking

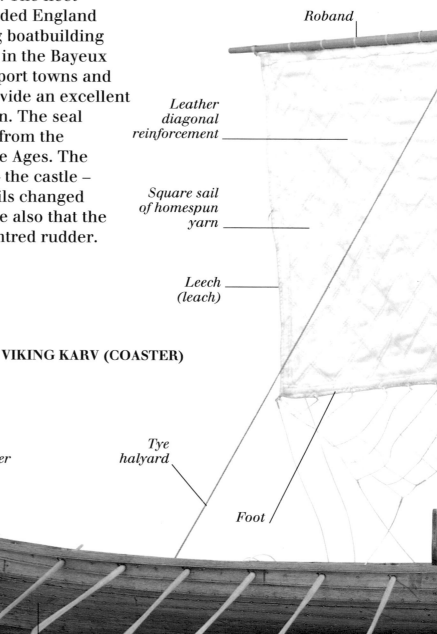

Zoomorphic head
Eye
Tooth

Braiding
Serpentine neck
Lozenge-shaped recess
Rectangular cross-band

DRAGON PROWHEAD

Snake-tail ornament

VIKING KARV (COASTER)

Sternpost
Boss (rudder pivot)
Steering oar (side rudder)
Tiller
Oar
Starboard (steerboard) side

Roband
Leather diagonal reinforcement
Square sail of homespun yarn
Leech (leach)
Tye halyard
Foot
Keel

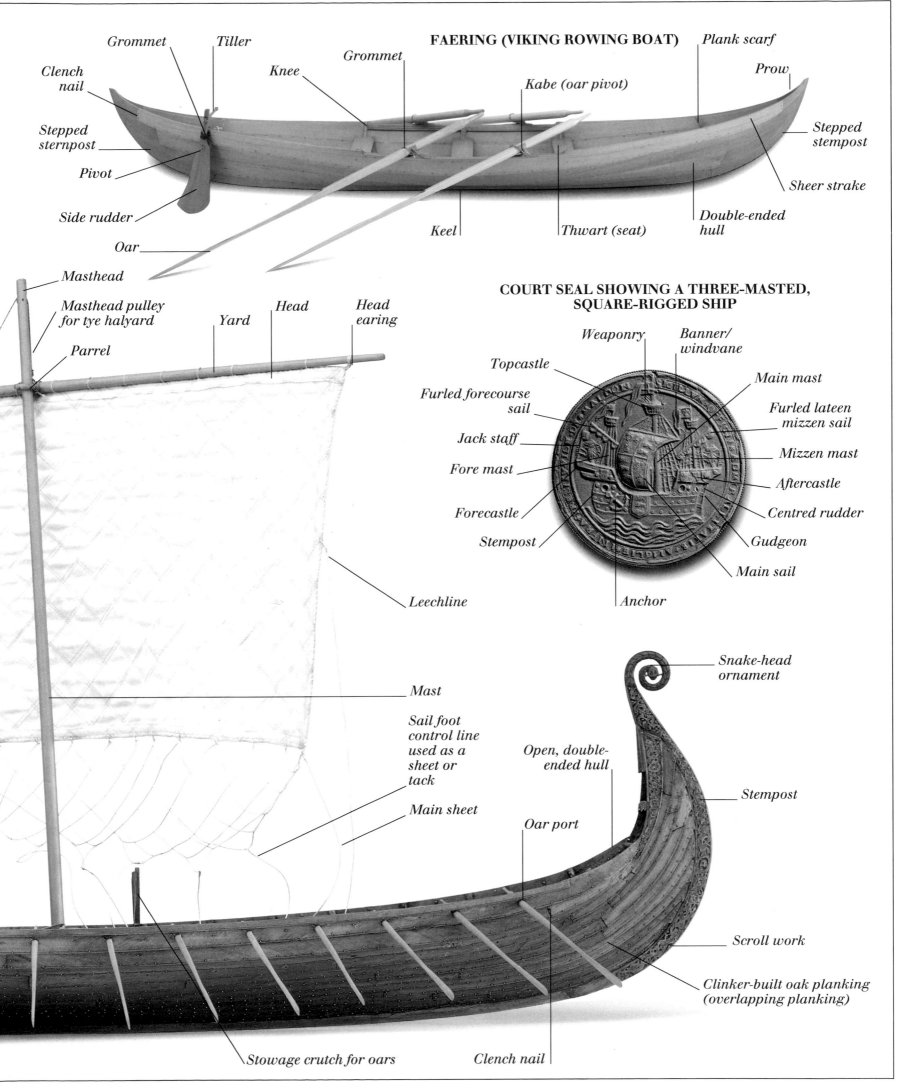

FAERING (VIKING ROWING BOAT)

Grommet

Tiller

Clench nail

Knee

Grommet

Stepped sternpost

Kabe (oar pivot)

Plank scarf

Prow

Stepped stempost

Pivot

Side rudder

Sheer strake

Oar

Keel

Thwart (seat)

Double-ended hull

Masthead

Masthead pulley for tye halyard

Yard

Head

Head earing

Parrel

COURT SEAL SHOWING A THREE-MASTED, SQUARE-RIGGED SHIP

Weaponry

Banner/ windvane

Topcastle

Main mast

Furled forecourse sail

Furled lateen mizzen sail

Jack staff

Mizzen mast

Fore mast

Aftercastle

Forecastle

Centred rudder

Stempost

Gudgeon

Anchor

Main sail

Leechline

Mast

Snake-head ornament

Sail foot control line used as a sheet or tack

Open, double-ended hull

Stempost

Main sheet

Oar port

Scroll work

Clinker-built oak planking (overlapping planking)

Stowage crutch for oars

Clench nail

Ships for war and trade

F ROM THE 16 TH CENTURY, SHIPS WERE BUILT WITH A NEW FORM OF HULL, constructed from carvel (edge-to-edge) planking. Warships of the time, like King Henry VIII of England's Mary Rose, boasted awesome fire power. This ship carried both long-range cannon in bronze, and short-range, anti-personnel guns in iron. Elsewhere, ships took on a multiformity of shapes. Dhows transported slaves from East Africa to Arabia, their fore-and-aft rigged lateen sails allowing them to sail close to the wind around the lands of the Indian Ocean. The Chinese sailed to East Africa and Arabia in junks, trading goods that were carried in watertight compartments. New astronomical tools helped medieval sailors to find their way. Cross-staves and astrolabes were used to measure the altitude of the sun or stars. One of a choice of four cross-pieces was slid up or down the staff of the cross-stave – which was graduated in degrees of altitude – until its top aligned with the celestial body and its base with the horizon. The sighting rule of the astrolabe was simply lined up with a known body, and its altitude read from marks on the metal disc. With sundials, the sailor could use the shadow of the sun to show the time of day.

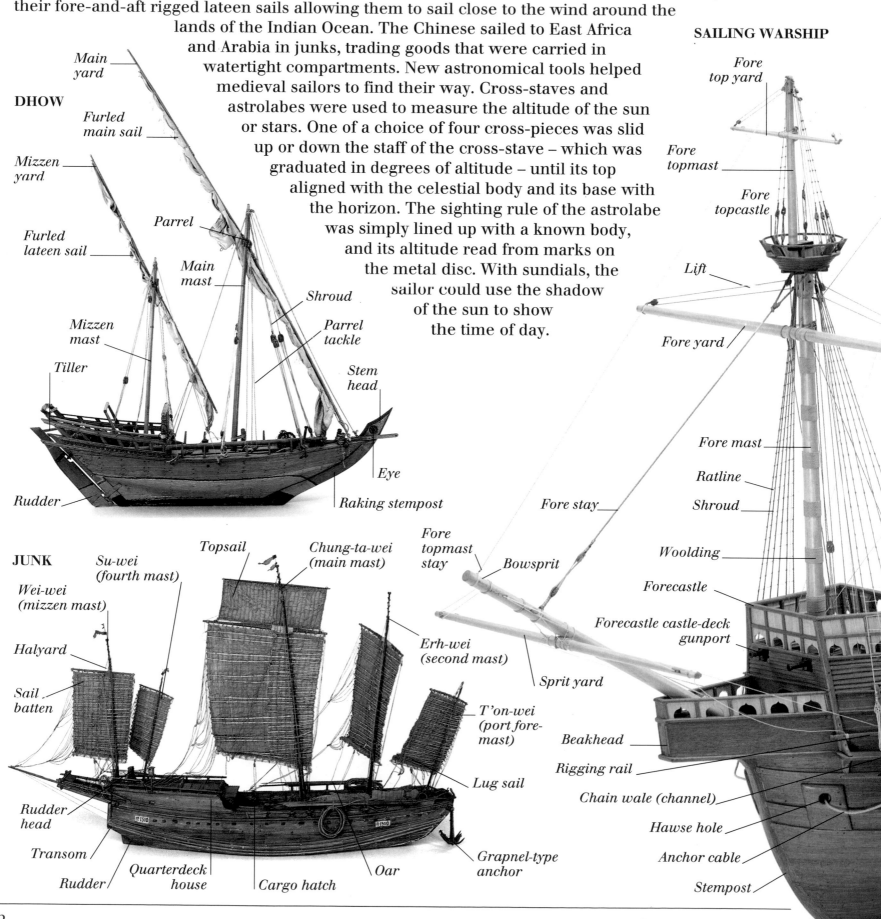

DHOW

Main yard

Furled main sail

Mizzen yard

Furled lateen sail

Parrel

Main mast

Mizzen mast

Shroud

Parrel tackle

Tiller

Stem head

Rudder

Eye

Raking stempost

SAILING WARSHIP

Fore top yard

Fore topmast

Fore topcastle

Lift

Fore yard

Fore mast

Ratline

Shroud

Woolding

Forecastle

Forecastle castle-deck gunport

Fore topmast stay

Bowsprit

Sprit yard

Fore stay

Beakhead

Rigging rail

Chain wale (channel)

Hawse hole

Anchor cable

Stempost

JUNK

Su-wei (fourth mast)

Topsail

Chung-ta-wei (main mast)

Wei-wei (mizzen mast)

Halyard

Sail batten

Erh-wei (second mast)

T'on-wei (port fore-mast)

Lug sail

Rudder head

Transom

Rudder

Quarterdeck house

Cargo hatch

Oar

Grapnel-type anchor

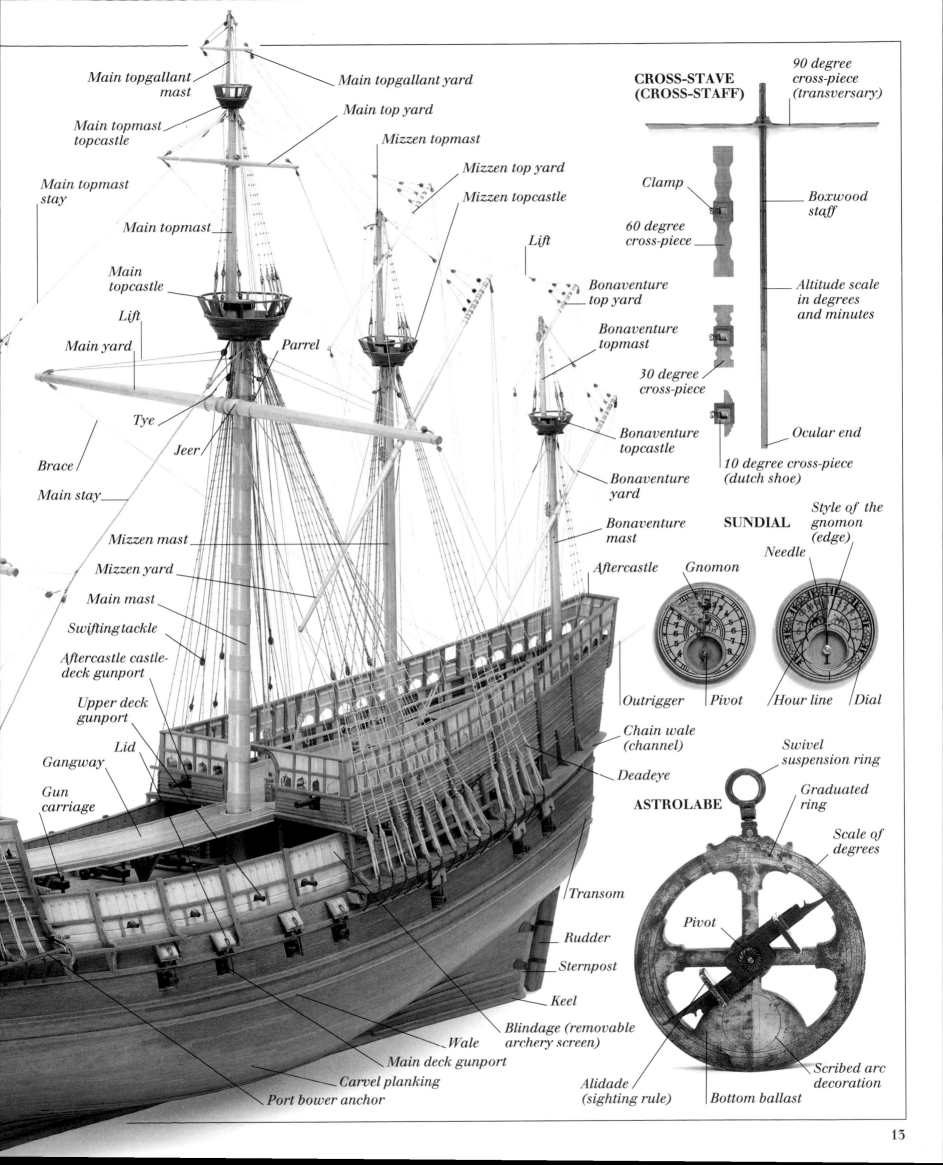

Main topgallant mast

Main topgallant yard

Main topmast topcastle

Main top yard

Mizzen topmast

Mizzen top yard

Main topmast stay

Mizzen topcastle

Main topmast

Lift

Main topcastle

Bonaventure top yard

Lift

Bonaventure topmast

Main yard

Parrel

Tye

Bonaventure topcastle

Jeer

Brace

Bonaventure yard

Main stay

Bonaventure mast

Mizzen mast

Aftercastle

Mizzen yard

Main mast

Swifting tackle

Aftercastle castle-deck gunport

Upper deck gunport

Chain wale (channel)

Lid

Deadeye

Gangway

Gun carriage

Transom

Rudder

Sternpost

Keel

Blindage (removable archery screen)

Wale

Main deck gunport

Carvel planking

Port bower anchor

CROSS-STAVE (CROSS-STAFF)

90 degree cross-piece (transversary)

Clamp

Boxwood staff

60 degree cross-piece

Altitude scale in degrees and minutes

30 degree cross-piece

Ocular end

10 degree cross-piece (dutch shoe)

SUNDIAL

Style of the gnomon (edge)

Needle

Gnomon

Outrigger

Pivot

Hour line

Dial

ASTROLABE

Swivel suspension ring

Graduated ring

Scale of degrees

Pivot

Alidade (sighting rule)

Bottom ballast

Scribed arc decoration

The expansion of sail

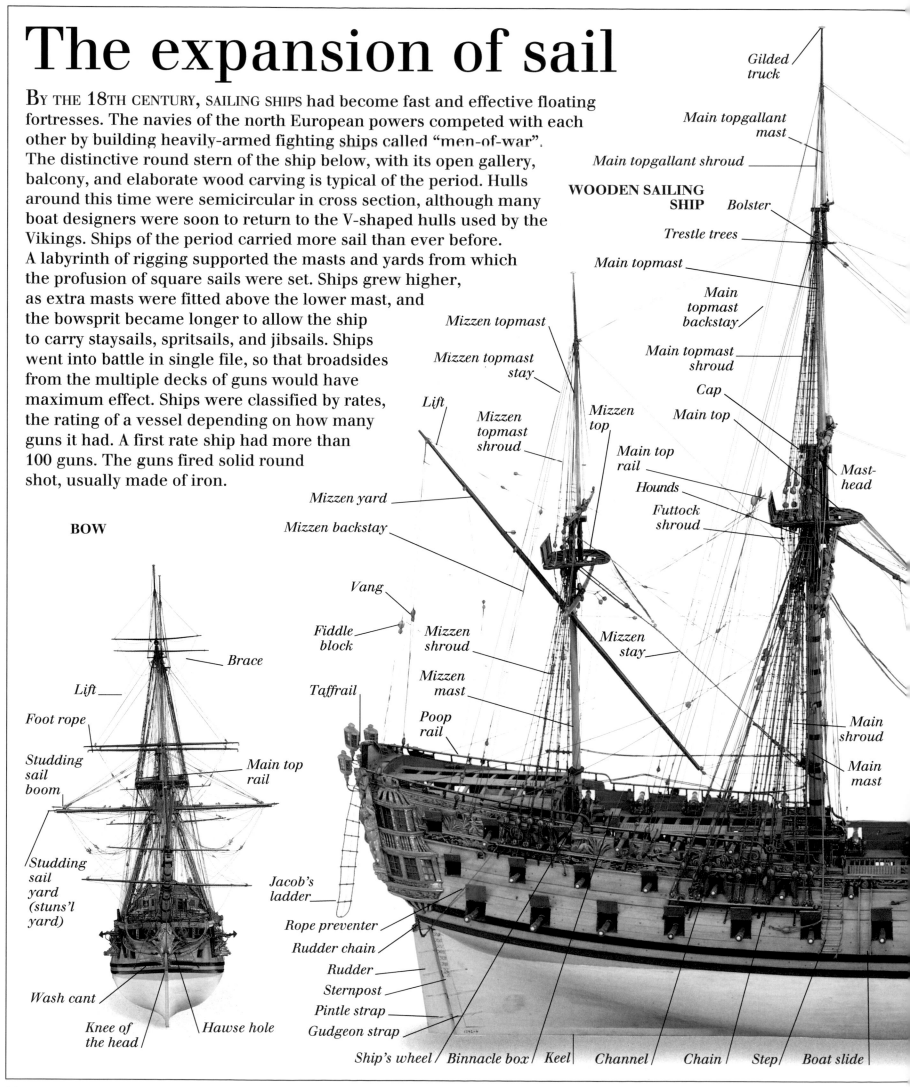

BY THE 18TH CENTURY, SAILING SHIPS had become fast and effective floating fortresses. The navies of the north European powers competed with each other by building heavily-armed fighting ships called "men-of-war". The distinctive round stern of the ship below, with its open gallery, balcony, and elaborate wood carving is typical of the period. Hulls around this time were semicircular in cross section, although many boat designers were soon to return to the V-shaped hulls used by the Vikings. Ships of the period carried more sail than ever before. A labyrinth of rigging supported the masts and yards from which the profusion of square sails were set. Ships grew higher, as extra masts were fitted above the lower mast, and the bowsprit became longer to allow the ship to carry staysails, spritsails, and jibsails. Ships went into battle in single file, so that broadsides from the multiple decks of guns would have maximum effect. Ships were classified by rates, the rating of a vessel depending on how many guns it had. A first rate ship had more than 100 guns. The guns fired solid round shot, usually made of iron.

Gilded truck

Main topgallant mast

Main topgallant shroud

WOODEN SAILING SHIP

Bolster

Trestle trees

Main topmast

Main topmast backstay

Main topmast shroud

Cap

Main top

Main top rail

Hounds

Futtock shroud

Mast-head

Mizzen topmast

Mizzen topmast stay

Lift

Mizzen topmast shroud

Mizzen top

Mizzen stay

Mizzen yard

Mizzen backstay

Vang

Fiddle block

Mizzen shroud

Mizzen mast

Taffrail

Poop rail

Main shroud

Main mast

BOW

Brace

Lift

Foot rope

Studding sail boom

Main top rail

Studding sail yard (stuns'l yard)

Jacob's ladder

Rope preventer

Rudder chain

Rudder

Sternpost

Pintle strap

Gudgeon strap

Wash cant

Knee of the head

Hawse hole

Ship's wheel Binnacle box Keel Channel Chain Step Boat slide

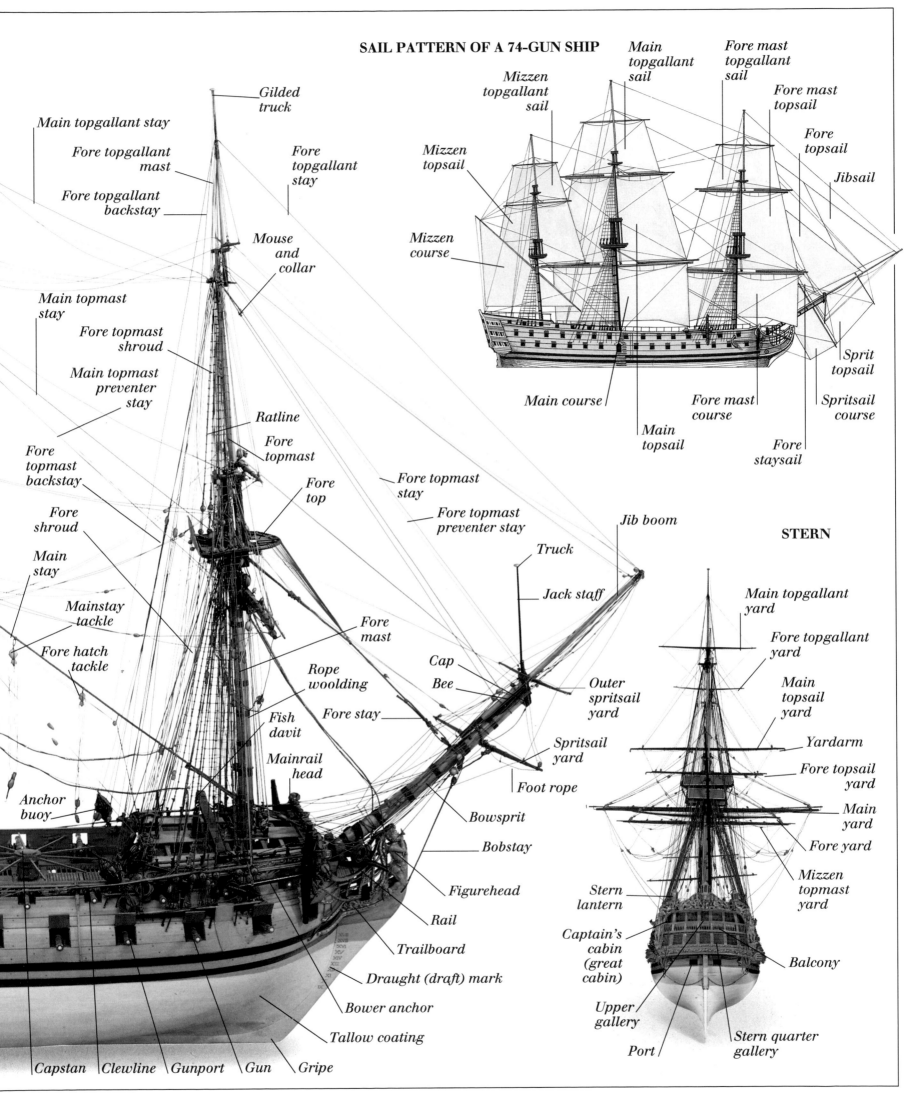

SAIL PATTERN OF A 74-GUN SHIP

Main topgallant stay

Fore topgallant mast

Fore topgallant backstay

Gilded truck

Fore topgallant stay

Mouse and collar

Mizzen topgallant sail

Main topgallant sail

Fore mast topgallant sail

Fore mast topsail

Mizzen topsail

Fore topsail

Mizzen course

Jibsail

Main topmast stay

Fore topmast shroud

Main topmast preventer stay

Ratline

Fore topmast

Sprit topsail

Fore topmast backstay

Fore top

Fore topmast stay

Fore topmast preventer stay

Main course

Fore mast course

Spritsail course

Main topsail

Fore staysail

Fore shroud

Main stay

Mainstay tackle

Fore hatch tackle

Fore mast

Rope woolding

Fore stay

Jib boom

Truck

Jack staff

Cap

Bee

Outer spritsail yard

STERN

Main topgallant yard

Fore topgallant yard

Fish davit

Mainrail head

Spritsail yard

Main topsail yard

Anchor buoy

Foot rope

Yardarm

Bowsprit

Fore topsail yard

Bobstay

Main yard

Figurehead

Fore yard

Rail

Stern lantern

Mizzen topmast yard

Trailboard

Captain's cabin (great cabin)

Balcony

Draught (draft) mark

Bower anchor

Tallow coating

Upper gallery

Port

Stern quarter gallery

Capstan   Clewline   Gunport   Gun   Gripe

A ship of the line

THE 74-GUN WOODEN SHIP WAS A MAINSTAY of British and French battlefleets in the late 18th and early 19th centuries. This "ship of the line" was heavy enough to fight with the most potent of rivals, yet nimble too. The length of such a ship was determined by the number of guns required for each deck, allowing enough room for crews to man them. The gun deck was about 52 m (170 ft) long. The decks had to be very strong to carry the weight of the guns. The deck planks have been removed on the vessel pictured below, to show just how close together the beams had to be to make the hull strong enough. Only timber with a perfect grain was used. The upper deck was open at the waist, but afore and abaft were officers' cabins. The forecastle and quarterdeck carried light guns and acted as platforms for working rigging and for reconnaissance. The ship's longboats (launches) were carried on booms between the gangways.

LONGBOAT

Truck
Mast
Jib halyard
Flag halyard
Backstay
Topping lift
Fore stay halyard
Peak halyard
Shroud
Main sheet
Fore sail halyard
Gaff
Boom
Parrel
Bowsprit
Traveller
Stempost
Deadeye
Oar
Side bench
Waterline

Thole pin
Windlass bar
Transom
Tiller
Planking
Rabbit line
Sheerplank
Frame
Keel
Rudder
Floor
Thwart (seat)

UPPER DECK OF A 74-GUN SHIP

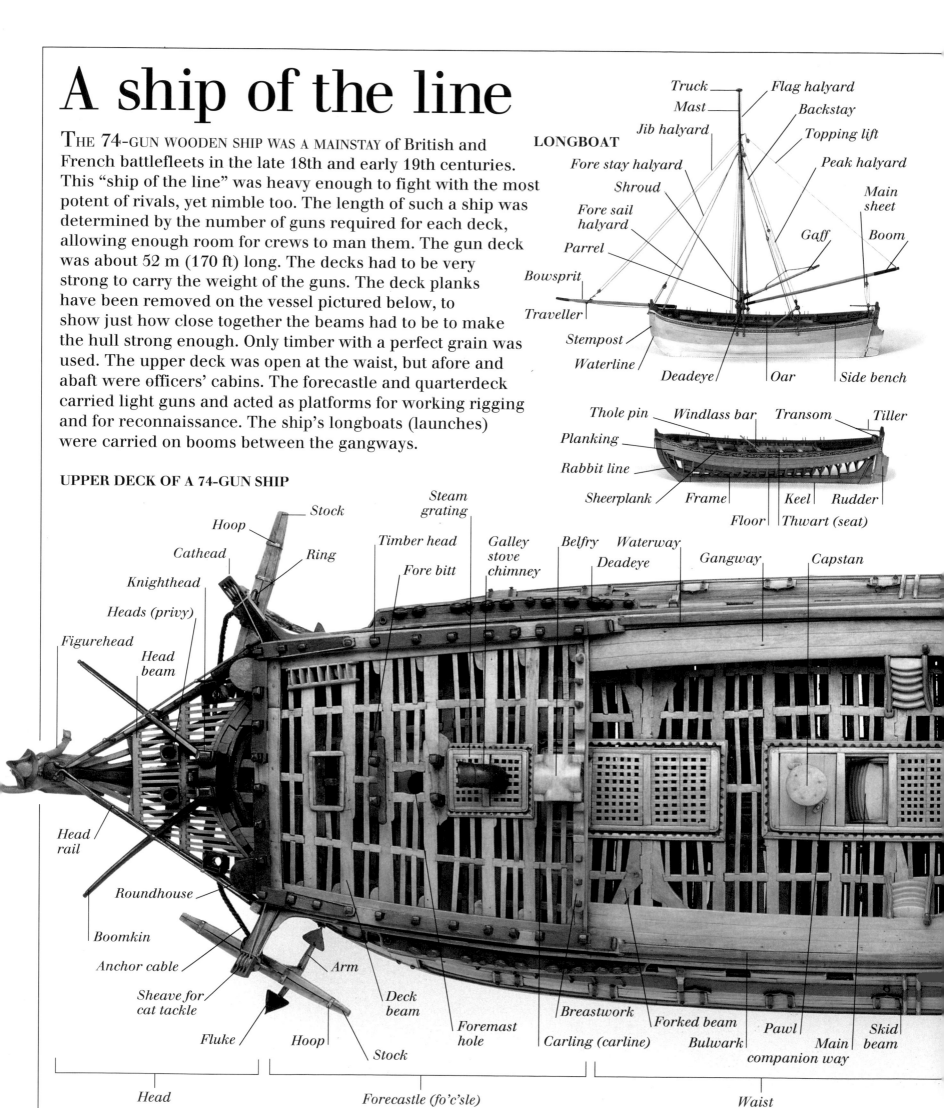

Stock
Hoop
Cathead
Ring
Knighthead
Heads (privy)
Figurehead
Head beam
Head rail
Roundhouse
Boomkin
Anchor cable
Sheave for cat tackle
Arm
Fluke
Hoop
Stock
Deck beam
Foremast hole
Timber head
Fore bitt
Steam grating
Galley stove chimney
Belfry
Deadeye
Waterway
Gangway
Capstan
Breastwork
Carling (carline)
Forked beam
Bulwark
Pawl
Main companion way
Skid beam

Head
Forecastle (fo'c'sle)
Waist

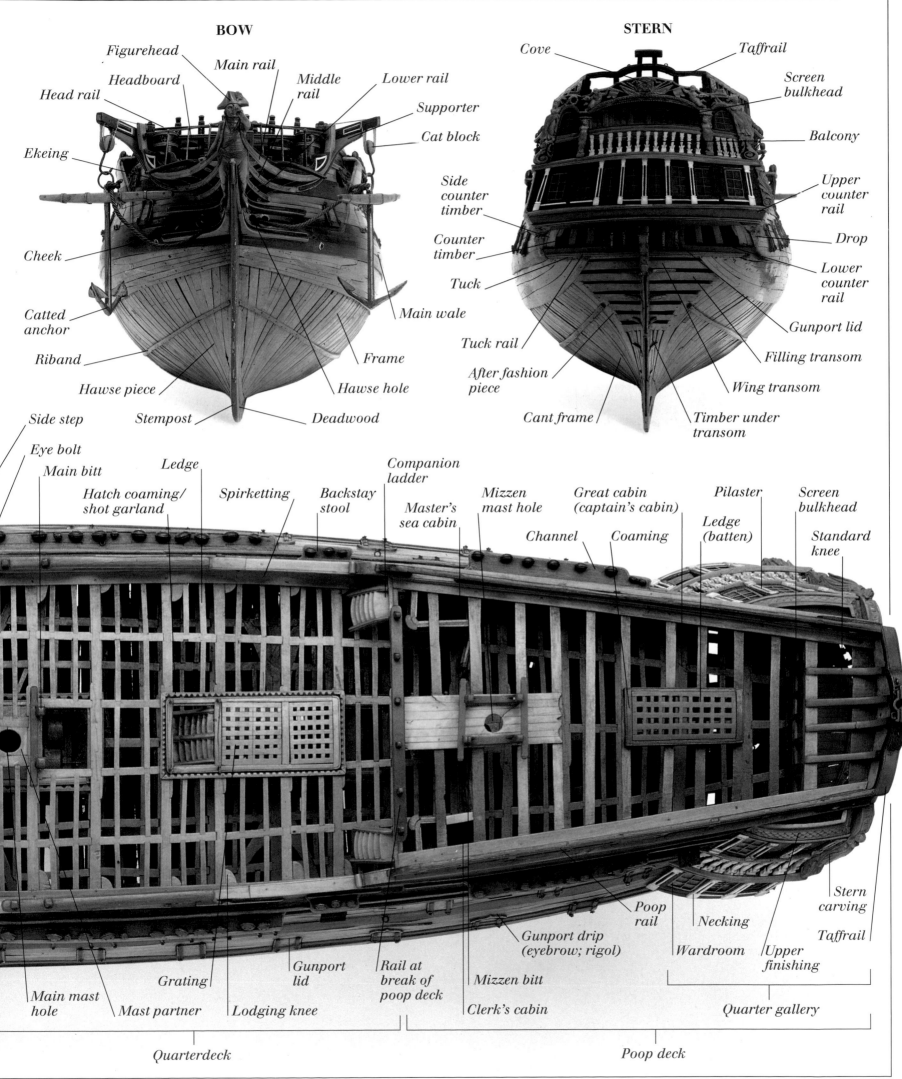

BOW

Figurehead

Main rail

Headboard

Middle rail

Head rail

Lower rail

Supporter

Cat block

Ekeing

Cheek

Catted anchor

Riband

Main wale

Hawse piece

Frame

Side step

Stempost

Hawse hole

Deadwood

STERN

Cove

Taffrail

Screen bulkhead

Balcony

Side counter timber

Upper counter rail

Counter timber

Drop

Lower counter rail

Tuck

Gunport lid

Tuck rail

Filling transom

After fashion piece

Wing transom

Cant frame

Timber under transom

Eye bolt

Main bitt

Ledge

Companion ladder

Mizzen mast hole

Great cabin (captain's cabin)

Pilaster

Screen bulkhead

Hatch coaming/ shot garland

Spirketting

Backstay stool

Master's sea cabin

Channel

Coaming

Ledge (batten)

Standard knee

Main mast hole

Mast partner

Grating

Lodging knee

Gunport lid

Rail at break of poop deck

Clerk's cabin

Mizzen bitt

Gunport drip (eyebrow; rigol)

Poop rail

Necking

Wardroom

Upper finishing

Stern carving

Taffrail

Quarter gallery

Quarterdeck

Poop deck

Anatomy of a wooden ship

THE SKELETON OF A WOODEN SHIP is a complex system of timbers joined together to form the frame, on which the planks and decks are attached. The many parts of a man-of-war's frame are laid out flat below to show the shape of each unit. (The old-fashioned terms for each piece of the frame are given.) The completed frame of a smaller craft, a collier brig, is shown opposite. Shipbuilders used wood from specially grown trees called "grown oaks" (right), whose limbs conformed naturally to the shapes needed for the knees, ryders, and other pieces that make up the frame. Water and heat were used to bend the oak to the final fit.

GROWN OAKS (COMPASS TIMBERS)

DISSECTION OF THE FRAME OF A MAN-OF-WAR

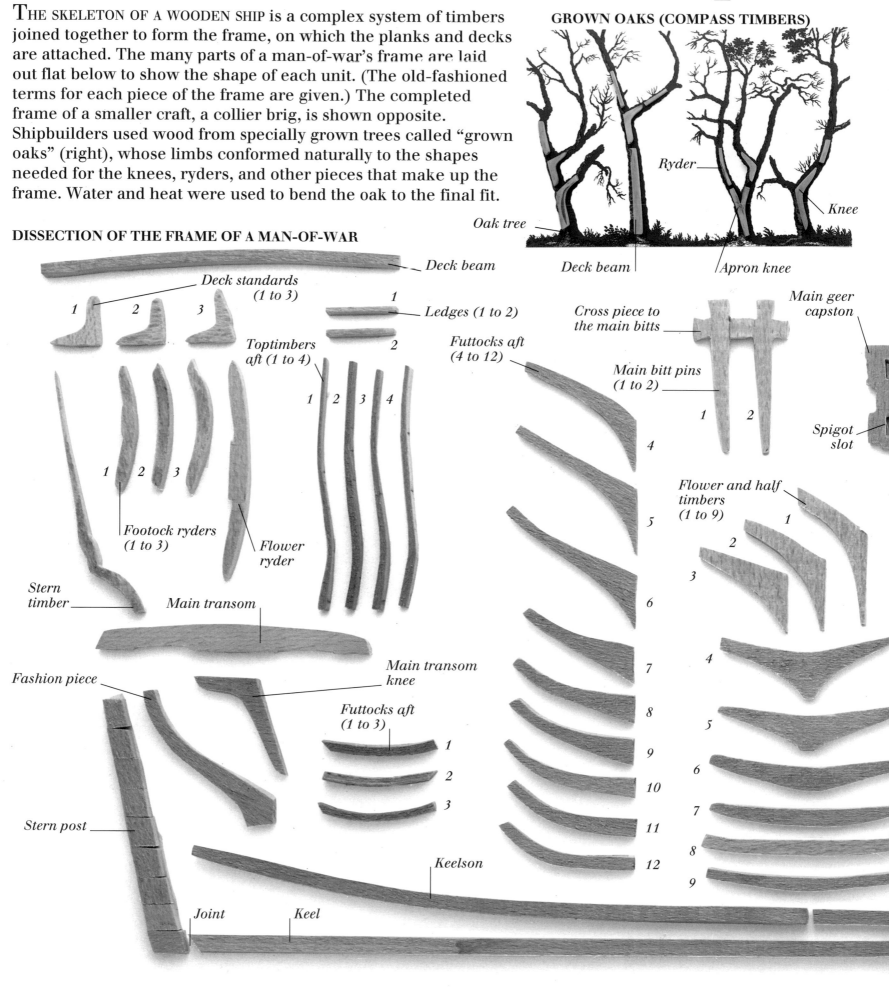

Ryder

Knee

Oak tree

Deck beam

Apron knee

Deck beam

Deck standards
(1 to 3)

1 2 3

Ledges (1 to 2)

1

2

Toptimbers
aft (1 to 4)

1 2 3 4

Futtocks aft
(4 to 12)

Cross piece to
the main bitts

Main geer
capston

Main bitt pins
(1 to 2)

1 2

Spigot
slot

Footock ryders
(1 to 3)

1 2 3

Flower
ryder

4

5

6

7

8

9

10

11

12

Flower and half
timbers
(1 to 9)

1

2

3

4

5

6

7

8

9

Stern
timber

Main transom

Main transom
knee

Futtocks aft
(1 to 3)

1

2

3

Fashion piece

Stern post

Keelson

Joint

Keel

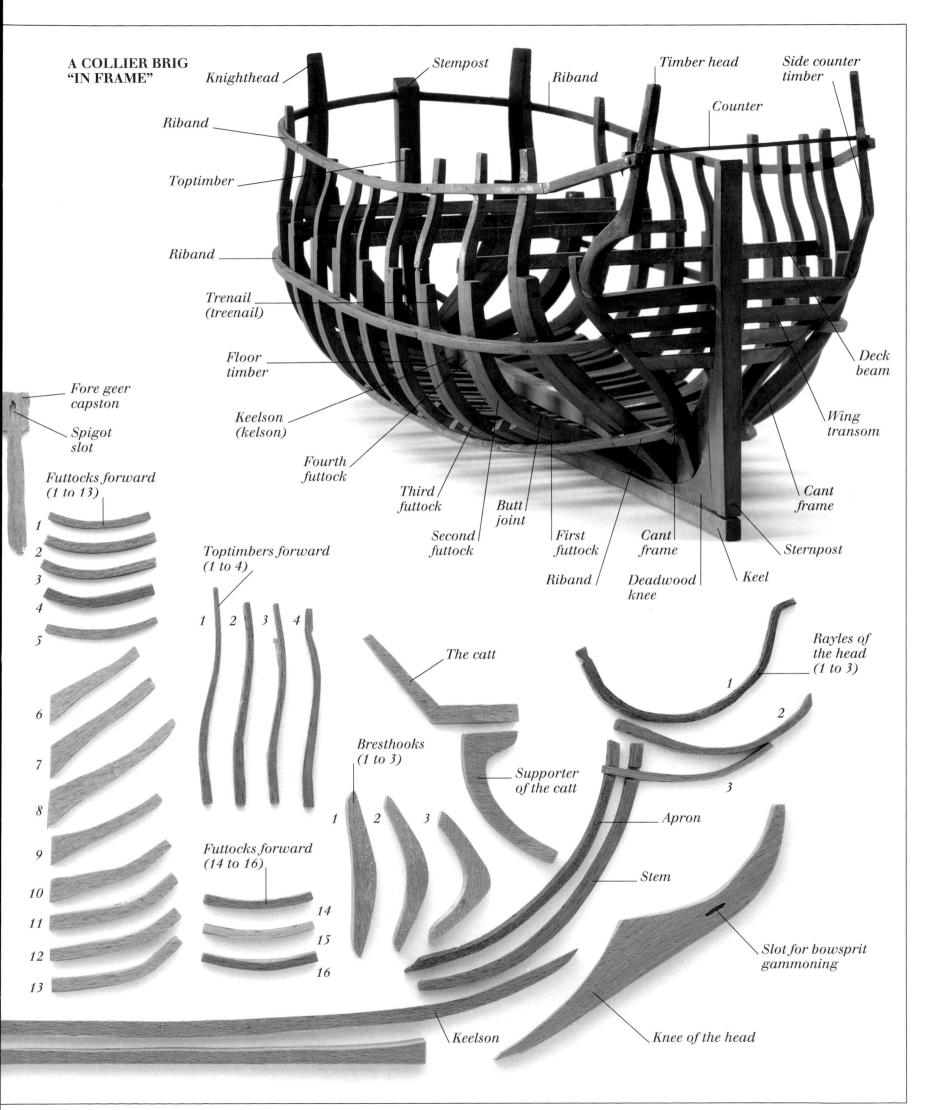

A COLLIER BRIG "IN FRAME"

Knighthead

Stempost

Riband

Timber head

Side counter timber

Riband

Counter

Toptimber

Riband

Deck beam

Trenail (treenail)

Floor timber

Fore geer capston

Keelson (kelson)

Wing transom

Spigot slot

Fourth futtock

Cant frame

Futtocks forward (1 to 13)

Third futtock

Butt joint

Second futtock

First futtock

Cant frame

Sternpost

1

Riband

Keel

2

Deadwood knee

3

Toptimbers forward (1 to 4)

The catt

Rayles of the head (1 to 3)

4

1   2   3   4

1

5

2

6

Bresthooks (1 to 3)

Supporter of the catt

3

7

8

1   2   3

Apron

9

Futtocks forward (14 to 16)

Stem

10

14

11

15

12

16

Slot for bowsprit gammoning

13

Keelson

Knee of the head

Anatomy of an iron ship

IRON PARTS WERE USED IN THE HULLS OF WOODEN SHIPS AS EARLY AS 1675, often in the same form as the wooden parts that they replaced. Eventually, as on the tea clipper Cutty Sark (below), iron rigging was found to be stronger than the traditional rope. The first "ironclads" were warships whose wooden hulls were protected by iron armour plates. Later ironclads actually had iron hulls. The model opposite is based on the British warship HMS Warrior, launched in 1860, the first battleship built entirely of iron. The plan of the iron paddlesteamer (bottom), built somewhat later, shows that this vessel was a sailing ship; but it also boasted a steam propulsion plant amidships that turned two side paddlewheels. Early iron hulls were made from plates that were painstakingly rivetted together (as below), but by the 20th century vessels began to be welded together, whole sections at a time. The Second World War "liberty ship" was one of the first of these "production-line vessels".

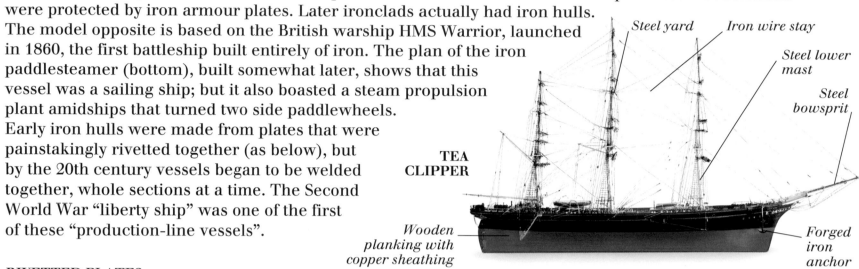

TEA CLIPPER

Steel yard

Iron wire stay

Steel lower mast

Steel bowsprit

Wooden planking with copper sheathing

Forged iron anchor

RIVETTED PLATES

Pan head rivet

Plate

Button head rivet (snap head)

Seam

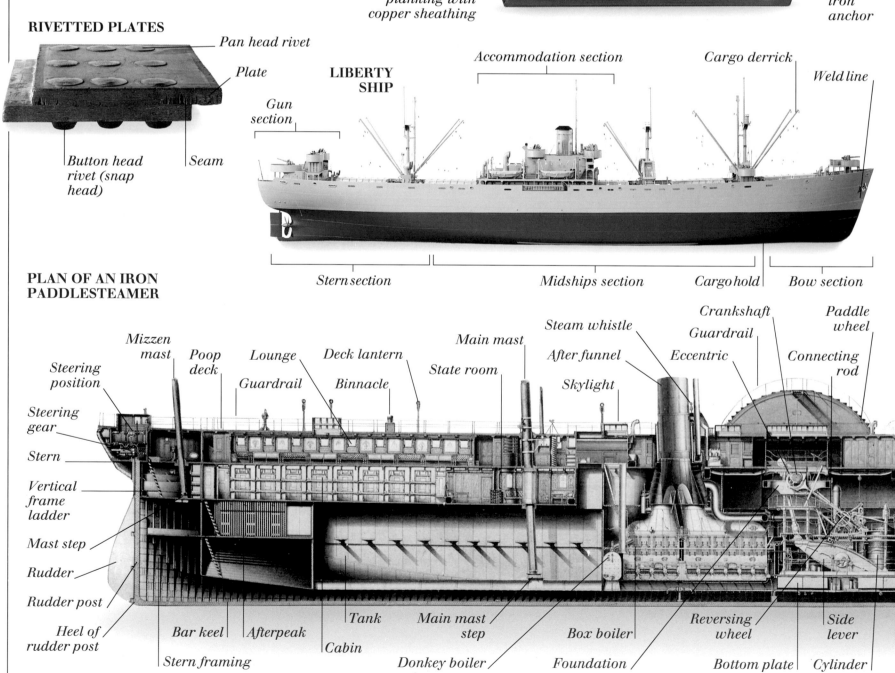

LIBERTY SHIP

Gun section

Accommodation section

Cargo derrick

Weld line

Stern section

Midships section

Cargo hold

Bow section

PLAN OF AN IRON PADDLESTEAMER

Steering position

Steering gear

Stern

Vertical frame ladder

Mast step

Rudder

Rudder post

Heel of rudder post

Mizzen mast

Poop deck

Lounge

Deck lantern

Guardrail

Binnacle

Main mast

State room

Steam whistle

After funnel

Skylight

Eccentric

Crankshaft

Guardrail

Connecting rod

Paddle wheel

Bar keel

Afterpeak

Cabin

Tank

Main mast step

Donkey boiler

Box boiler

Foundation

Reversing wheel

Bottom plate

Side lever

Cylinder

Stern framing

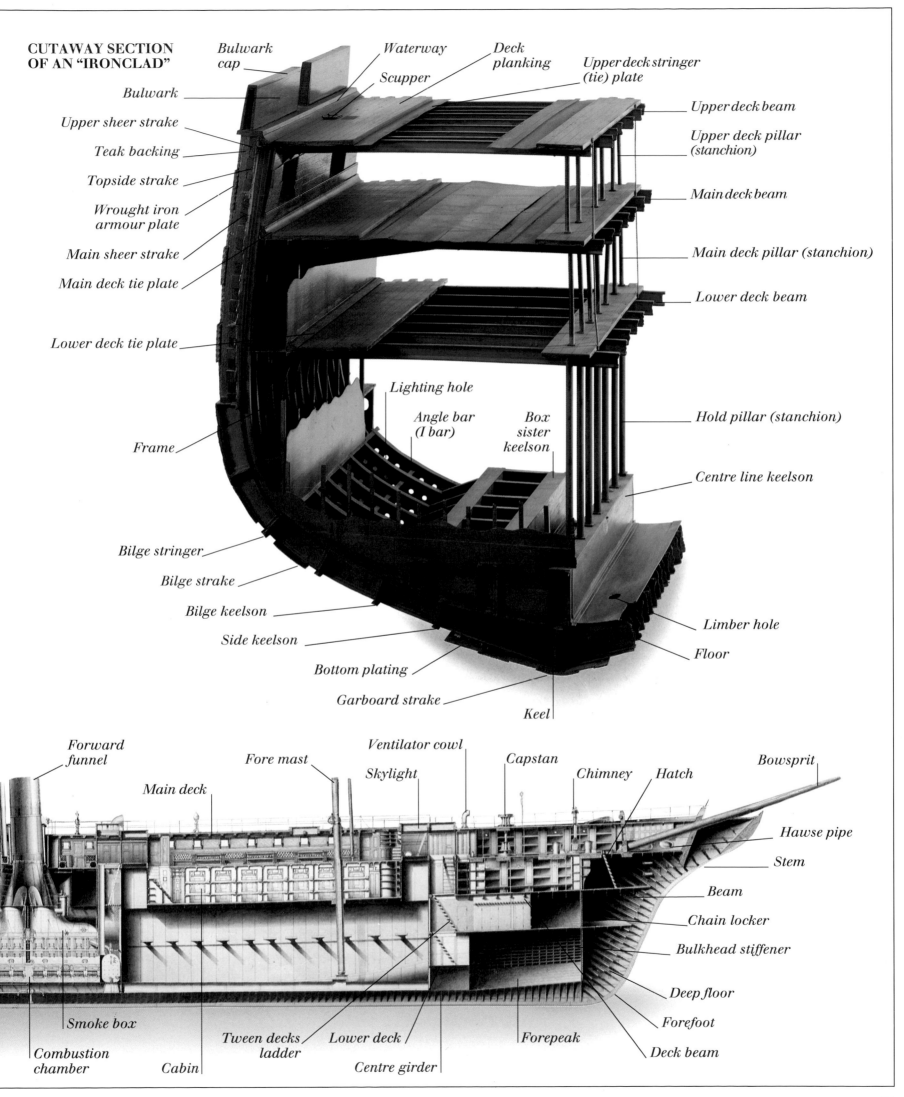

CUTAWAY SECTION OF AN "IRONCLAD"

Bulwark cap

Bulwark

Upper sheer strake

Teak backing

Topside strake

Wrought iron armour plate

Main sheer strake

Main deck tie plate

Lower deck tie plate

Frame

Bilge stringer

Bilge strake

Bilge keelson

Side keelson

Bottom plating

Garboard strake

Waterway

Scupper

Deck planking

Upper deck stringer (tie) plate

Upper deck beam

Upper deck pillar (stanchion)

Main deck beam

Main deck pillar (stanchion)

Lower deck beam

Lighting hole

Angle bar (I bar)

Box sister keelson

Hold pillar (stanchion)

Centre line keelson

Limber hole

Floor

Keel

Forward funnel

Main deck

Fore mast

Skylight

Ventilator cowl

Capstan

Chimney

Hatch

Bowsprit

Hawse pipe

Stem

Beam

Chain locker

Bulkhead stiffener

Deep floor

Forefoot

Deck beam

Smoke box

Combustion chamber

Cabin

Tween decks ladder

Lower deck

Centre girder

Forepeak

21

Paddle wheels and propellers

THE INVENTION OF THE STEAM ENGINE IN THE 18TH CENTURY made mechanically driven ships fitted with paddle wheels or propellers a viable alternative to sails. Paddle wheels have fixed or feathered floats, and the model shown below features both types. Feathered floats give more propulsive power than fixed floats because they are almost upright at all times in the water. Paddle wheels were superseded by the propeller on ocean-going vessels in the mid-19th century. Propellers are more efficient, work better in rough water, and are less vulnerable in collisions. The first propellers were two-bladed but later three- and four-bladed versions are more powerful; the shape and pitch of blades have also been refined over the years. At the beginning of the 18th century, tillers were superseded on many larger ships by the ship's wheel as a means of steering.

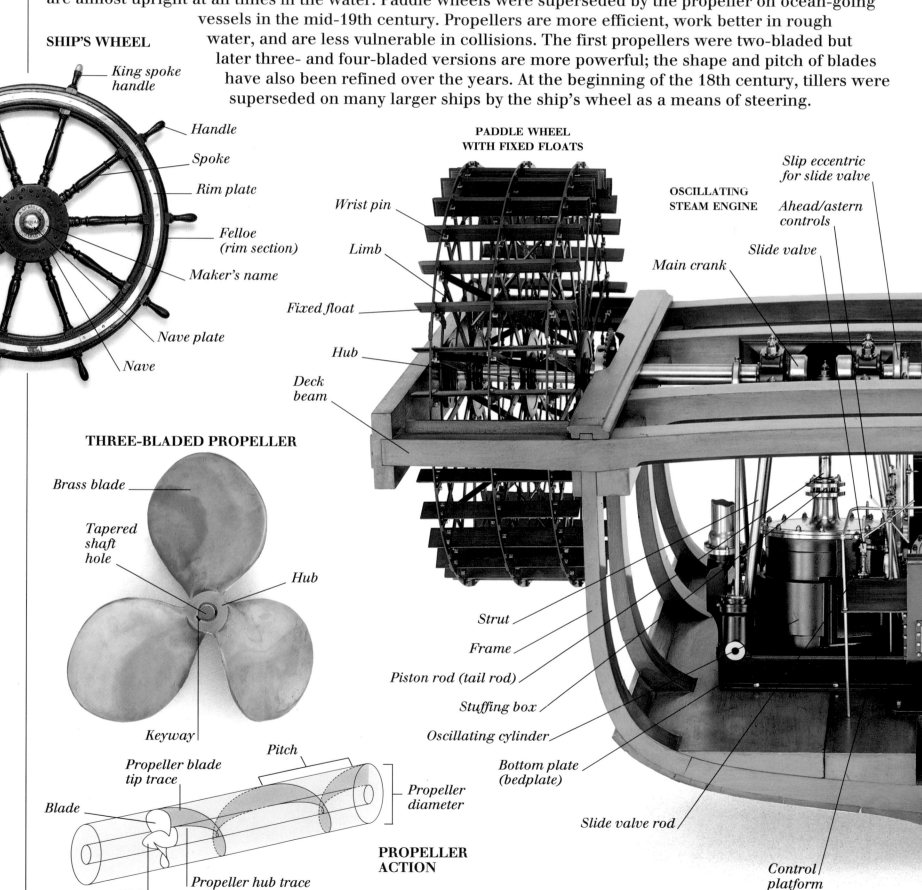

SHIP'S WHEEL

King spoke handle

Handle

Spoke

Rim plate

Felloe (rim section)

Maker's name

Nave plate

Nave

PADDLE WHEEL WITH FIXED FLOATS

Wrist pin

Limb

Fixed float

Hub

Deck beam

OSCILLATING STEAM ENGINE

Slip eccentric for slide valve

Ahead/astern controls

Slide valve

Main crank

THREE-BLADED PROPELLER

Brass blade

Tapered shaft hole

Hub

Keyway

Strut

Frame

Piston rod (tail rod)

Stuffing box

Oscillating cylinder

Bottom plate (bedplate)

Slide valve rod

Control platform

Propeller blade tip trace

Pitch

Blade

Propeller diameter

Hub

Propeller hub trace

PROPELLER ACTION

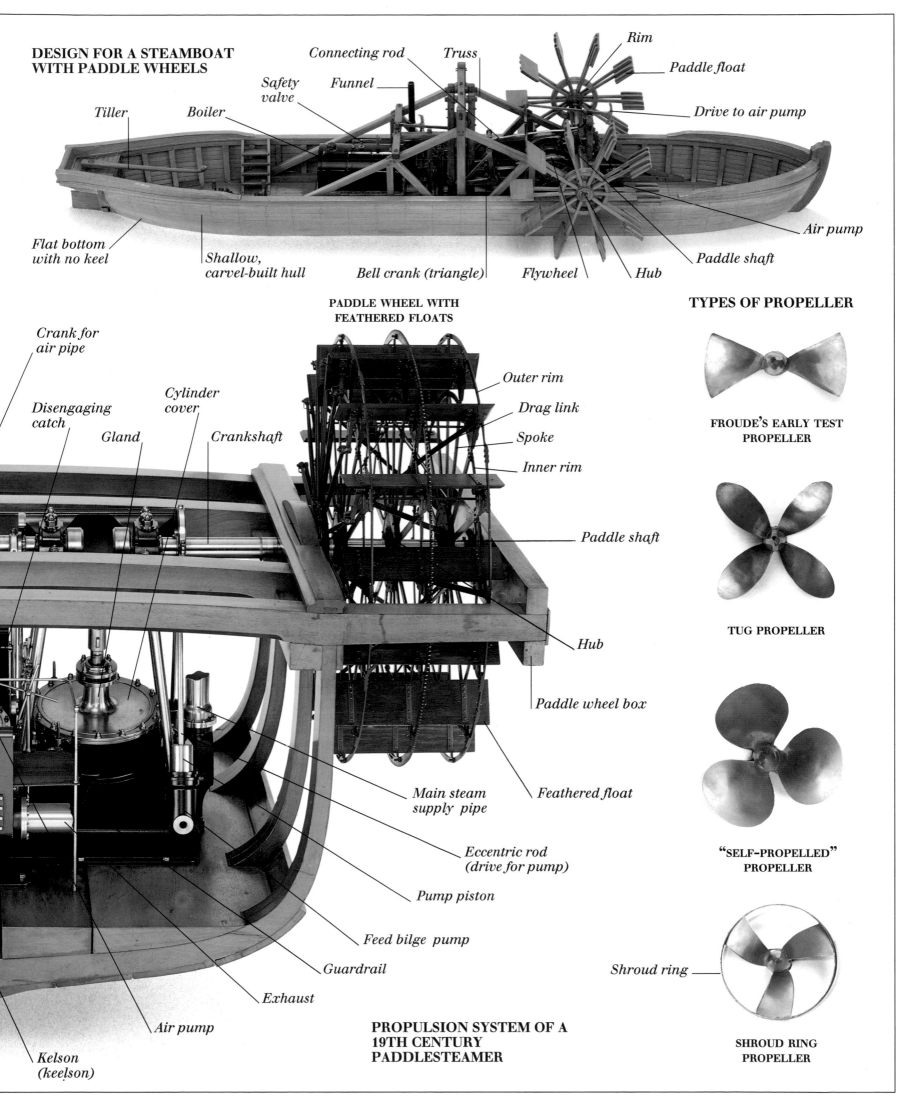

DESIGN FOR A STEAMBOAT WITH PADDLE WHEELS

Connecting rod

Truss

Rim

Paddle float

Safety valve

Funnel

Drive to air pump

Tiller

Boiler

Flat bottom with no keel

Shallow, carvel-built hull

Bell crank (triangle)

Flywheel

Hub

Paddle shaft

Air pump

TYPES OF PROPELLER

PADDLE WHEEL WITH FEATHERED FLOATS

Crank for air pipe

Disengaging catch

Cylinder cover

Gland

Crankshaft

Outer rim

Drag link

Spoke

Inner rim

Paddle shaft

Hub

Paddle wheel box

Main steam supply pipe

Feathered float

Eccentric rod (drive for pump)

Pump piston

Feed bilge pump

Guardrail

Exhaust

Air pump

Kelson (keelson)

PROPULSION SYSTEM OF A 19TH CENTURY PADDLESTEAMER

FROUDE'S EARLY TEST PROPELLER

TUG PROPELLER

"SELF-PROPELLED" PROPELLER

Shroud ring

SHROUD RING PROPELLER

The boatbuilder's yard

TRADITIONALLY, MOST SMALL BOATS have been built in a painstaking manner; by laboriously softening and shaping hardwoods, and by fastening the planking (strakes) with copper rivets. Modern boats, in contrast, are often built with readily available materials, such as plywood, resin, and synthetic rope and cloth. The dinghy shown here is clinker-built (having overlapping strakes) but, unlike older clinker boats – on which the strakes are laid down first – it is made up around a jig (positional guide), and is very quick to assemble.

OARS

Peek cringle

Peek (peak)

Loom

BOATBUILDING JIG

Gunwhale

Inwale

Transom knee (quarter knee)

Daggerboard case

Thwart knee

Seat support

Seat support

Oar hole

Grooved reinforcement pad

Apron knee

Mast step

Mast hole

Grooved reinforcement pad

Leech (leach)

Stern transom

Rudder

Station mould

Strongback (backbone)

Bow transom

Thwart knee

Station mould

Shaft

Transom knee (quarter knee)

Tiller

Apron knee

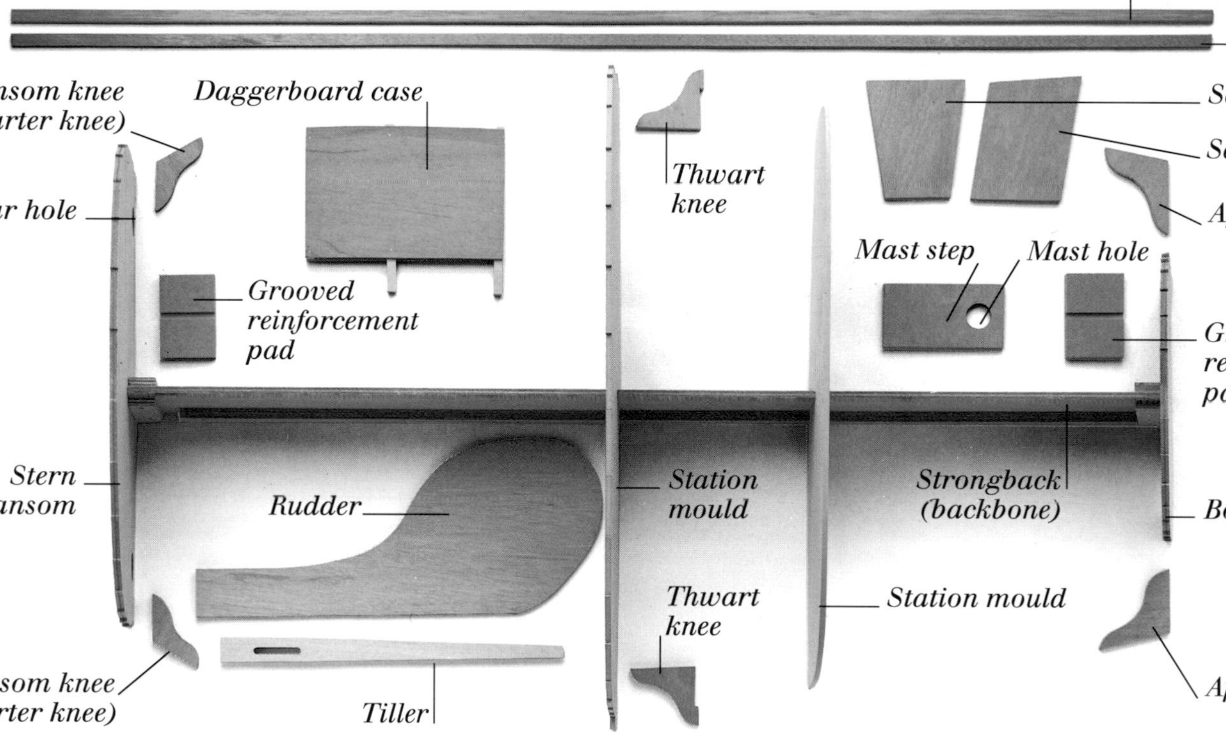

PLANKING FOR ONE SIDE OF THE DINGHY

Daggerboard slot

Keel

Blade

Garboard strake

Matched edges

Bilge strake

Clew

Clew cringle

Separating edges

Middle strakes

Main sheet

Convex taper

Concave taper

Upper strakes

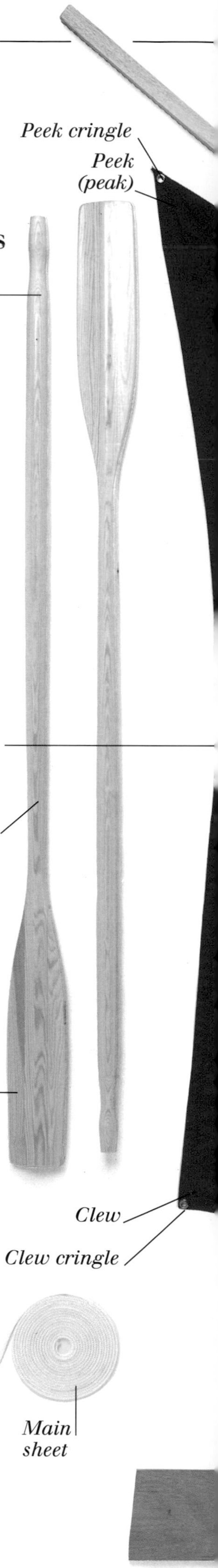

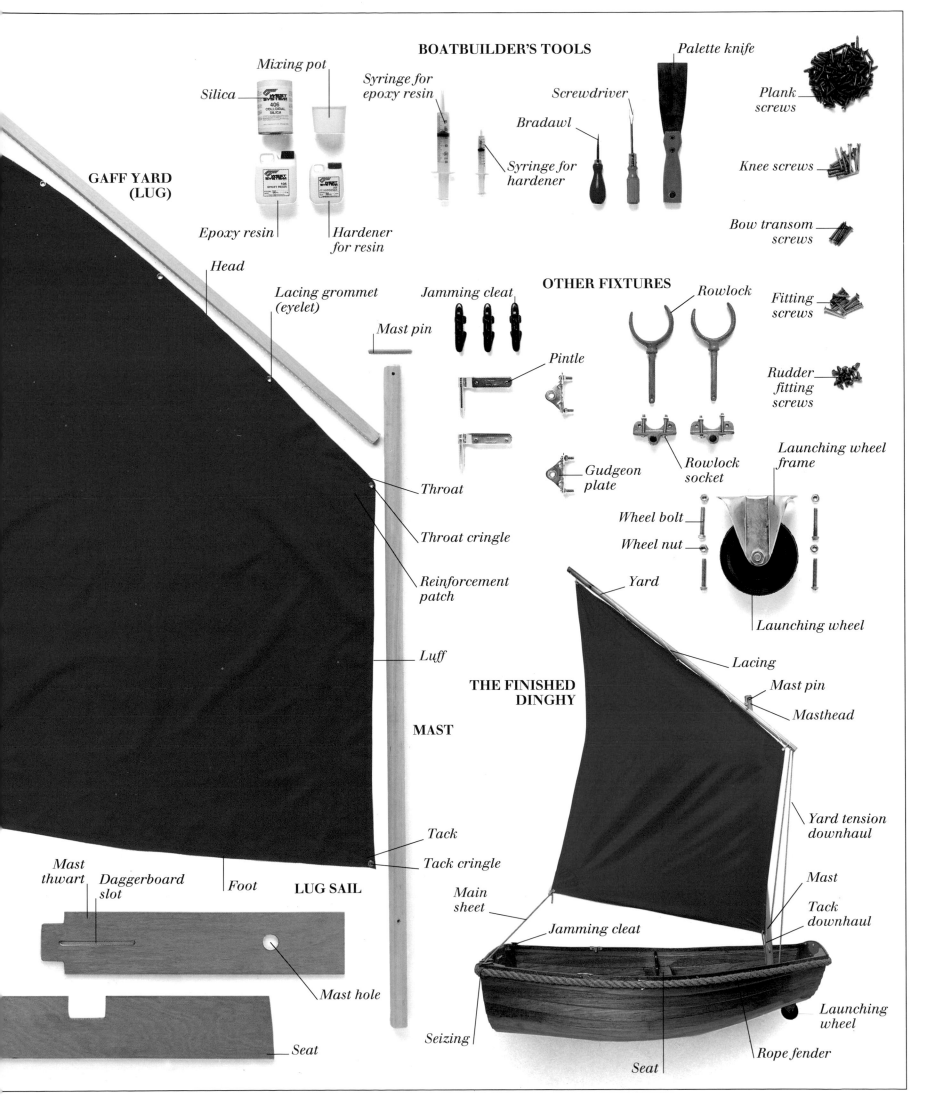

BOATBUILDER'S TOOLS

Mixing pot

Silica

Syringe for epoxy resin

Palette knife

Screwdriver

Bradawl

Plank screws

Syringe for hardener

Knee screws

Epoxy resin

Hardener for resin

Bow transom screws

GAFF YARD (LUG)

Head

Lacing grommet (eyelet)

OTHER FIXTURES

Jamming cleat

Rowlock

Fitting screws

Mast pin

Pintle

Rudder fitting screws

Throat

Throat cringle

Gudgeon plate

Rowlock socket

Launching wheel frame

Wheel bolt

Wheel nut

Yard

Reinforcement patch

Launching wheel

Luff

Lacing

THE FINISHED DINGHY

Mast pin

Masthead

MAST

Yard tension downhaul

Tack

Tack cringle

Main sheet

Mast

Mast thwart

Daggerboard slot

Foot

LUG SAIL

Jamming cleat

Tack downhaul

Mast hole

Seizing

Launching wheel

Seat

Seat

Rope fender

Rigging

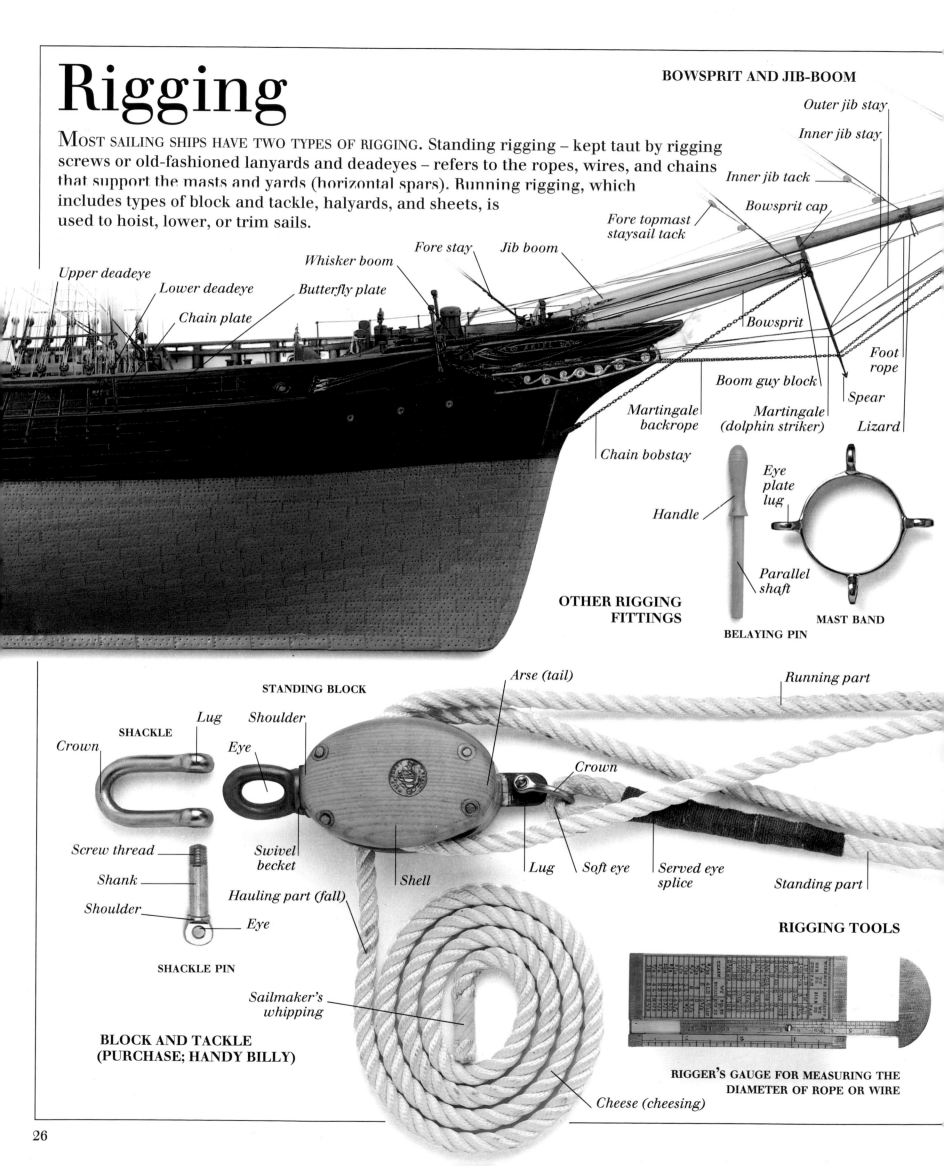

Most sailing ships have two types of rigging. Standing rigging – kept taut by rigging screws or old-fashioned lanyards and deadeyes – refers to the ropes, wires, and chains that support the masts and yards (horizontal spars). Running rigging, which includes types of block and tackle, halyards, and sheets, is used to hoist, lower, or trim sails.

BOWSPRIT AND JIB-BOOM

Outer jib stay

Inner jib stay

Inner jib tack

Bowsprit cap

Fore topmast
staysail tack

Fore stay

Whisker boom

Jib boom

Upper deadeye

Lower deadeye

Butterfly plate

Chain plate

Bowsprit

Foot
rope

Boom guy block

Spear

Martingale
backrope

Martingale
(dolphin striker)

Lizard

Chain bobstay

**OTHER RIGGING
FITTINGS**

Handle

Eye
plate
lug

Parallel
shaft

MAST BAND

BELAYING PIN

STANDING BLOCK

Arse (tail)

Running part

SHACKLE

Lug

Shoulder

Crown

Eye

Crown

Screw thread

Swivel
becket

Lug

Soft eye

Served eye
splice

Standing part

Shank

Shell

Shoulder

Eye

Hauling part (fall)

RIGGING TOOLS

SHACKLE PIN

Sailmaker's
whipping

**BLOCK AND TACKLE
(PURCHASE; HANDY BILLY)**

Cheese (cheesing)

**RIGGER'S GAUGE FOR MEASURING THE
DIAMETER OF ROPE OR WIRE**

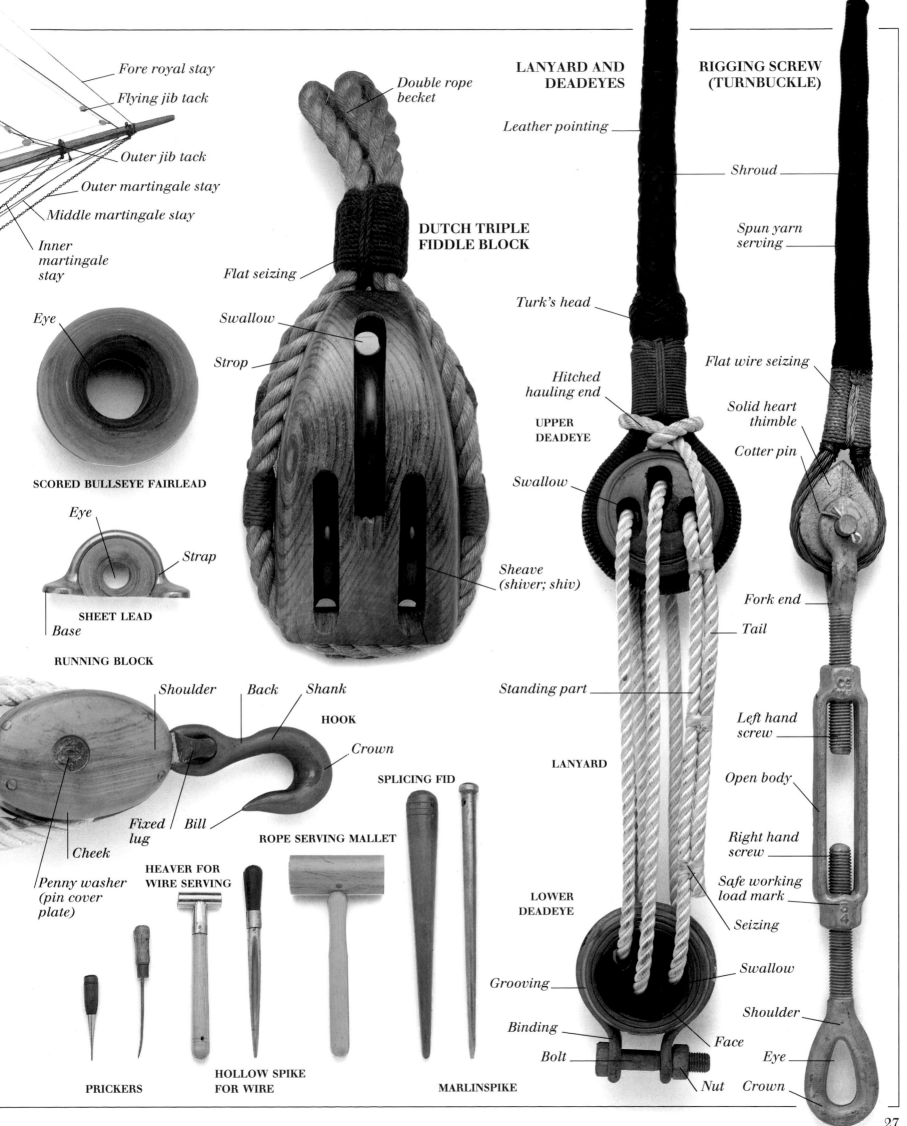

Fore royal stay

Flying jib tack

Outer jib tack

Outer martingale stay

Middle martingale stay

Inner
martingale
stay

Double rope
becket

**LANYARD AND
DEADEYES**

**RIGGING SCREW
(TURNBUCKLE)**

Leather pointing

Shroud

Spun yarn
serving

**DUTCH TRIPLE
FIDDLE BLOCK**

Flat seizing

Swallow

Strop

Eye

SCORED BULLSEYE FAIRLEAD

Eye

Strap

SHEET LEAD

Base

RUNNING BLOCK

Turk's head

Hitched
hauling end

**UPPER
DEADEYE**

Swallow

Sheave
(shiver; shiv)

Flat wire seizing

Solid heart
thimble

Cotter pin

Fork end

Tail

Standing part

Shoulder   Back   Shank

HOOK

Crown

LANYARD

Left hand
screw

Open body

Right hand
screw

Fixed
lug

Bill

SPLICING FID

ROPE SERVING MALLET

Safe working
load mark

Cheek

Penny washer
(pin cover
plate)

**HEAVER FOR
WIRE SERVING**

**LOWER
DEADEYE**

Seizing

Swallow

Grooving

Binding

Bolt

Face

Shoulder

Eye

PRICKERS

**HOLLOW SPIKE
FOR WIRE**

MARLINSPIKE

Nut   Crown

Sails

THERE ARE TWO MAIN TYPES OF SAIL, often used in combination. Square sails are driving sails. They are usually attached by parrels to yards, square to the mast to catch the following wind. On fore-and-aft sails, such as lateen and lug sails, the luff (leading edge) usually abuts a mast or a stay. The head of the sail may abut a gaff, and the foot a boom. Around the world, a great range of rigs (sail patterns), such as the ketch, lugger, and schooner, has evolved to suit local needs. Sails are made from strips of cloth, cut to give the sail a belly and strong enough to resist the most violent of winds. Cotton and flax are the traditional sail materials, but synthetic fabrics are now commonly used.

SECTION OF A SAIL

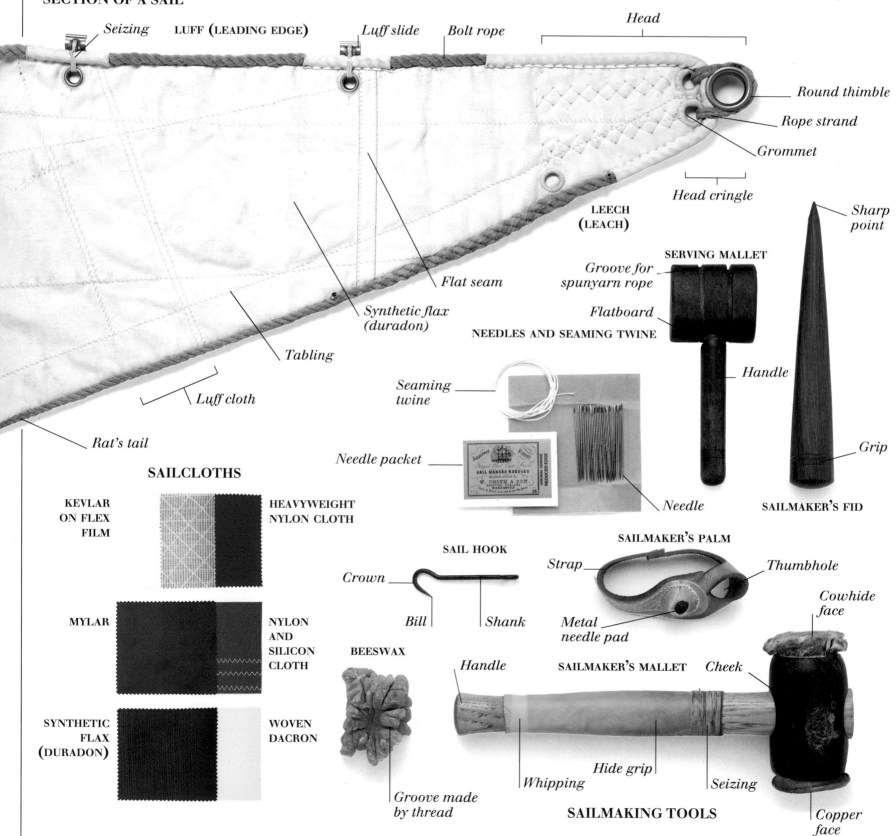

Seizing LUFF (LEADING EDGE) Luff slide Bolt rope Head Round thimble Rope strand Grommet Head cringle LEECH (LEACH) Flat seam Synthetic flax (duradon) Tabling Luff cloth Rat's tail

SERVING MALLET Sharp point Groove for spunyarn rope Flatboard Handle Grip SAILMAKER'S FID

NEEDLES AND SEAMING TWINE Seaming twine Needle packet Needle

SAILCLOTHS

KEVLAR ON FLEX FILM HEAVYWEIGHT NYLON CLOTH

MYLAR NYLON AND SILICON CLOTH

SYNTHETIC FLAX (DURADON) WOVEN DACRON

SAIL HOOK Crown Bill Shank

SAILMAKER'S PALM Strap Thumbhole Metal needle pad

BEESWAX Groove made by thread

Handle Whipping Hide grip **SAILMAKER'S MALLET** Cheek Seizing Cowhide face Copper face

SAILMAKING TOOLS

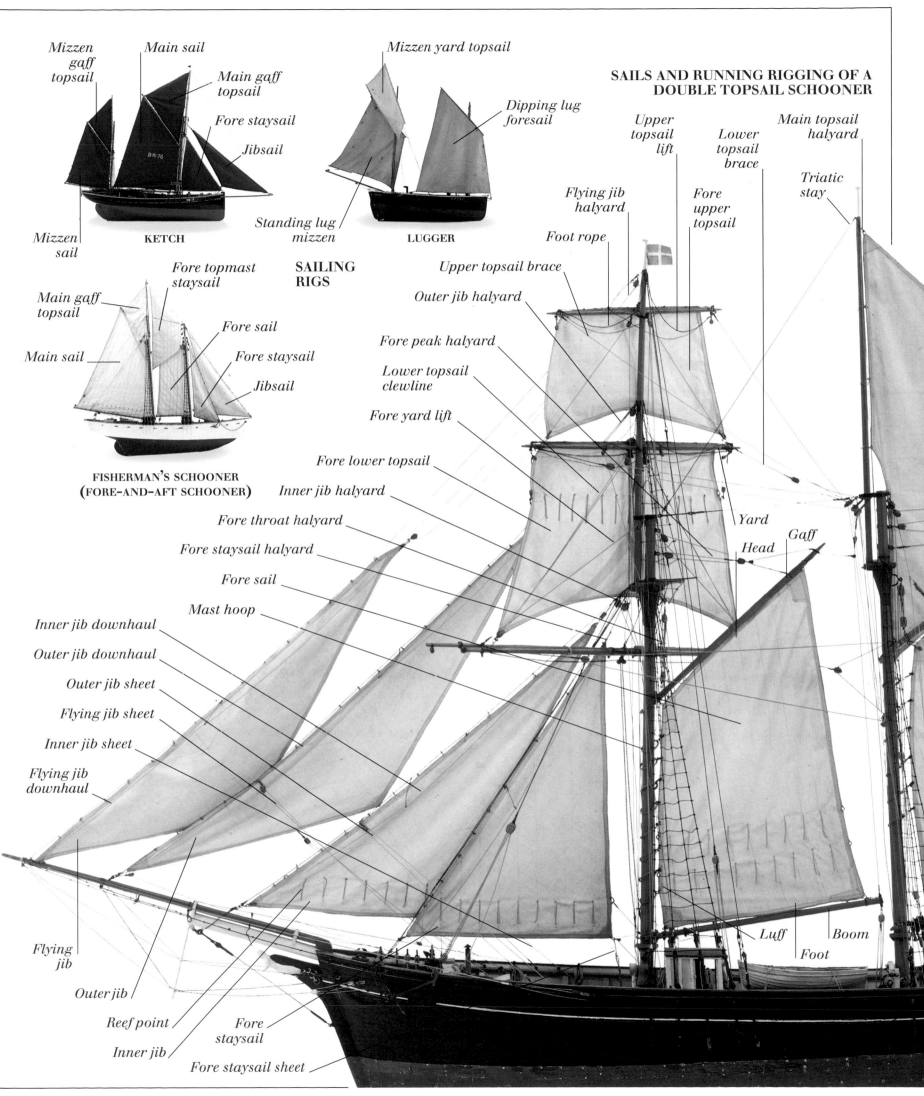

Mizzen gaff topsail

Main sail

Main gaff topsail

Fore staysail

Jibsail

Mizzen sail

KETCH

Mizzen yard topsail

Dipping lug foresail

Standing lug mizzen

LUGGER

SAILS AND RUNNING RIGGING OF A DOUBLE TOPSAIL SCHOONER

Upper topsail lift

Lower topsail brace

Main topsail halyard

Triatic stay

Flying jib halyard

Fore upper topsail

Foot rope

Main gaff topsail

Fore topmast staysail

SAILING RIGS

Upper topsail brace

Outer jib halyard

Main sail

Fore sail

Fore staysail

Jibsail

Fore peak halyard

Lower topsail clewline

Fore yard lift

FISHERMAN'S SCHOONER (FORE-AND-AFT SCHOONER)

Fore lower topsail

Inner jib halyard

Yard

Head

Gaff

Fore throat halyard

Fore staysail halyard

Fore sail

Mast hoop

Inner jib downhaul

Outer jib downhaul

Outer jib sheet

Flying jib sheet

Inner jib sheet

Flying jib downhaul

Luff

Boom

Foot

Flying jib

Outer jib

Reef point

Fore staysail

Inner jib

Fore staysail sheet

29

Man-powered craft

WHILE MANY MAN-POWERED CRAFT HAVE CHANGED LITTLE since the first boats, others have been developed for specific purposes, such as carrying goods, fishing, and sport. The cargo-carrying Bangladeshi dinghy is paddled or punted with a pole. The coracle is used for fishing. It is paddled over the bow with one hand only, the other hand being needed to work the fishing net. A rowing boat is rowed with a continuous cycle of strokes. To row a boat with a pair of oars is known as "sculling". Water is prevented from entering the hull of a sculling boat by a canvas that is pulled tight between the in-boards. The racing boat below has had its canvases removed so that the frame can be seen. Oars are levered around a crutch or gate. The canoe opposite has an outrigger to keep it from turning over.

CRUTCHES

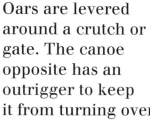

Captive socket

Pintle

Shoulder

Crutch plate

TURNOVER ROWLOCK   **UNEVEN ROWLOCK**   **SQUARE PATTERN ROWLOCK**

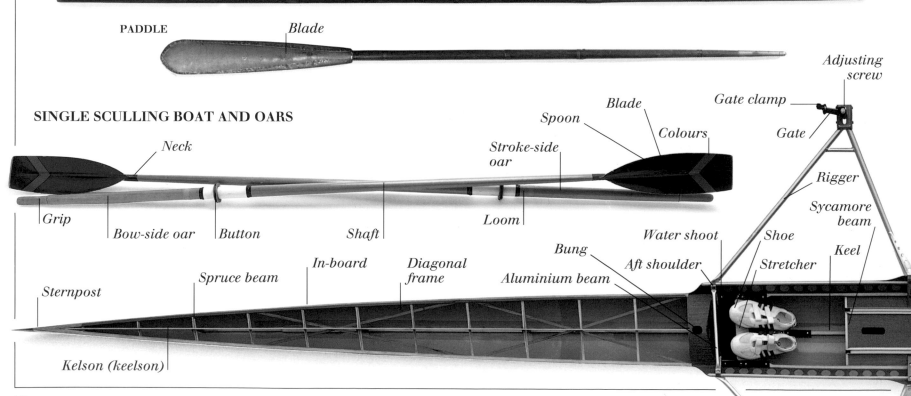

Quarter oar for steering

Stern

Goloi

Quarter oar pivot

Tie for quarter oar pivot

Woven split bamboo deck cover

BANGLADESHI DINGHY

POLE

PADDLE   *Blade*

SINGLE SCULLING BOAT AND OARS

Neck

Blade

Spoon

Colours

Stroke-side oar

Gate clamp

Adjusting screw

Gate

Rigger

Grip

Bow-side oar   *Button*   *Shaft*   *Loom*

Sycamore beam

Water shoot   *Shoe*   *Keel*

Bung   *Aft shoulder*   *Stretcher*

Sternpost

Spruce beam   *In-board*   *Diagonal frame*   *Aluminium beam*

Kelson (keelson)

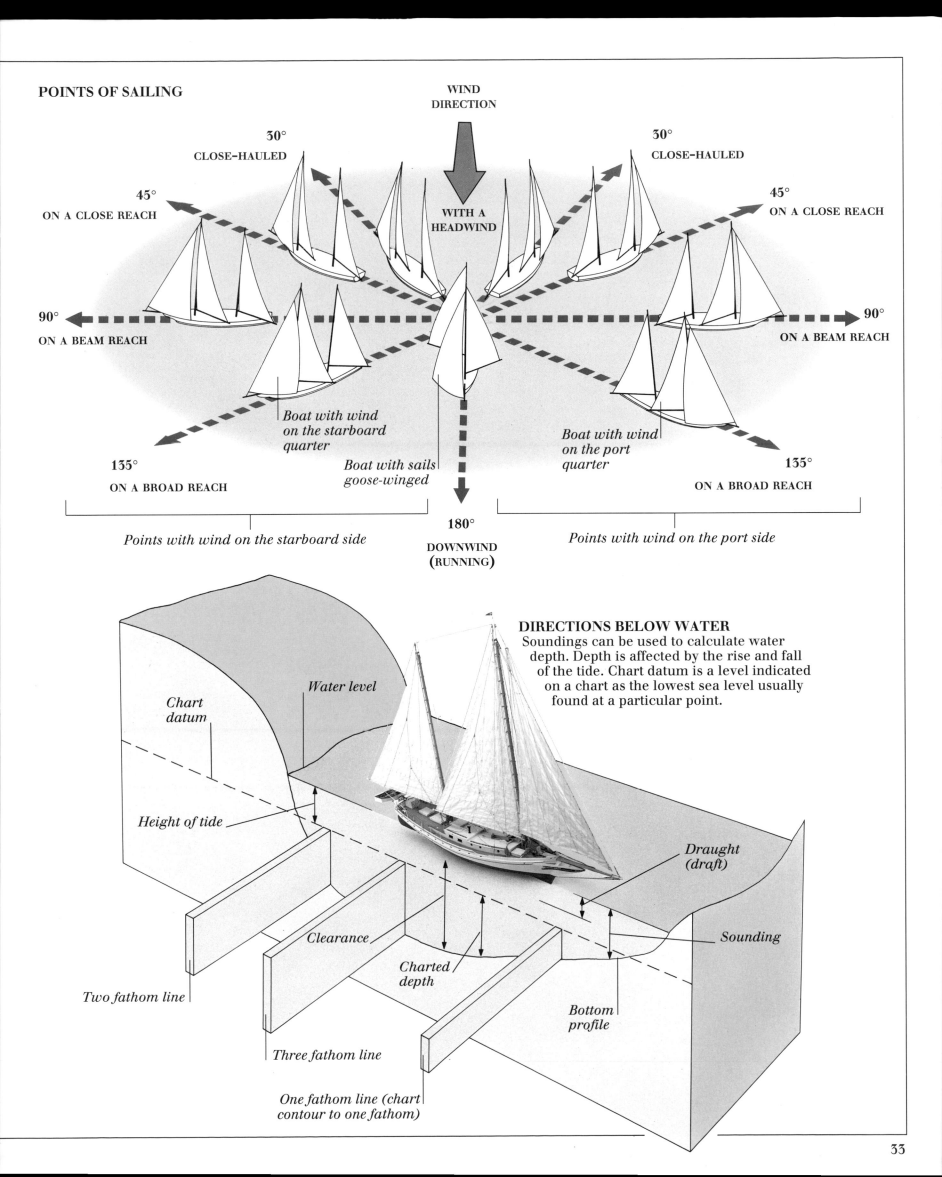

POINTS OF SAILING

WIND DIRECTION

30° CLOSE-HAULED

30° CLOSE-HAULED

45° ON A CLOSE REACH

45° ON A CLOSE REACH

WITH A HEADWIND

90° ON A BEAM REACH

90° ON A BEAM REACH

Boat with wind on the starboard quarter

Boat with wind on the port quarter

Boat with sails goose-winged

135° ON A BROAD REACH

135° ON A BROAD REACH

Points with wind on the starboard side

Points with wind on the port side

180° DOWNWIND (RUNNING)

DIRECTIONS BELOW WATER

Soundings can be used to calculate water depth. Depth is affected by the rise and fall of the tide. Chart datum is a level indicated on a chart as the lowest sea level usually found at a particular point.

Water level

Chart datum

Height of tide

Draught (draft)

Sounding

Clearance

Charted depth

Bottom profile

Two fathom line

Three fathom line

One fathom line (chart contour to one fathom)

Navigation

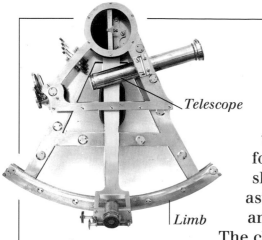

Telescope

Limb

EARLY SEXTANT

NAVIGATION IS THE ART OF TAKING A SHIP SAFELY between two points defined in terms of their latitude and longitude. Sailors in early times relied on landmarks for direction, while the watchkeeper turned an hourglass to indicate how long the ship had been following a given compass course. Like the cross-stave and the astrolabe, the sextant enabled sailors to measure their latitude by showing the angle between two known objects, or between a heavenly body and the horizon. The chronometer allowed the mariner to calculate longitude accurately, by comparing local time with the time at Greenwich (0° longitude). Speed and distance were found in open seas by trailing astern a patent log, as shown opposite.

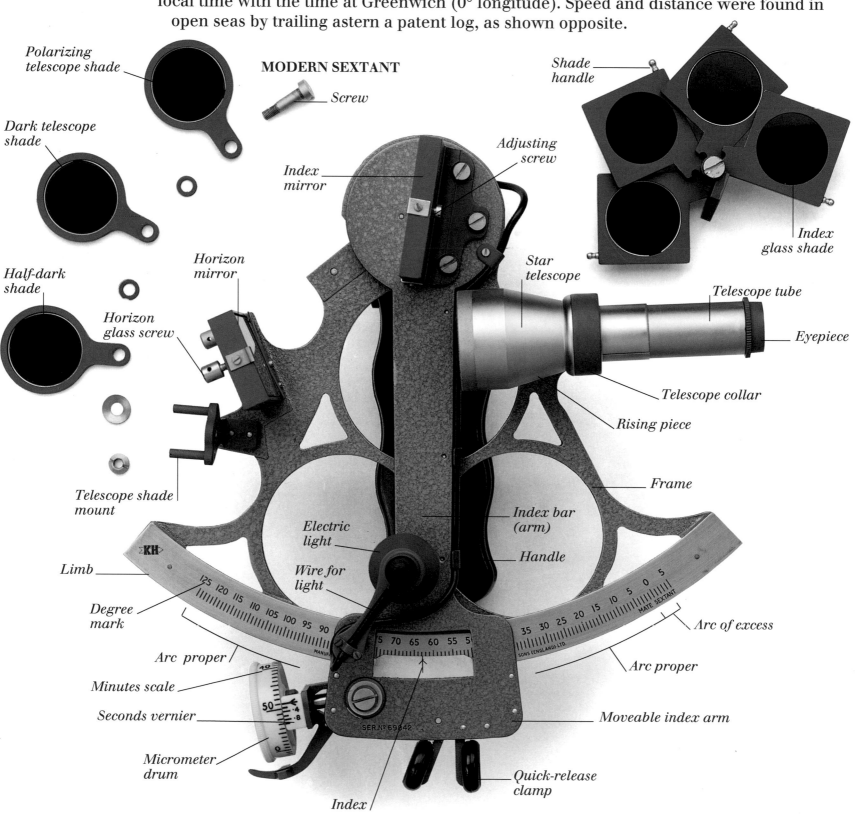

Polarizing telescope shade

Dark telescope shade

MODERN SEXTANT

Screw

Shade handle

Index mirror

Adjusting screw

Star telescope

Index glass shade

Half-dark shade

Horizon mirror

Telescope tube

Horizon glass screw

Eyepiece

Telescope collar

Rising piece

Frame

Telescope shade mount

Index bar (arm)

Electric light

Handle

Limb

Wire for light

Degree mark

Arc of excess

Arc proper

Arc proper

Minutes scale

Seconds vernier

Moveable index arm

Micrometer drum

Index

Quick-release clamp

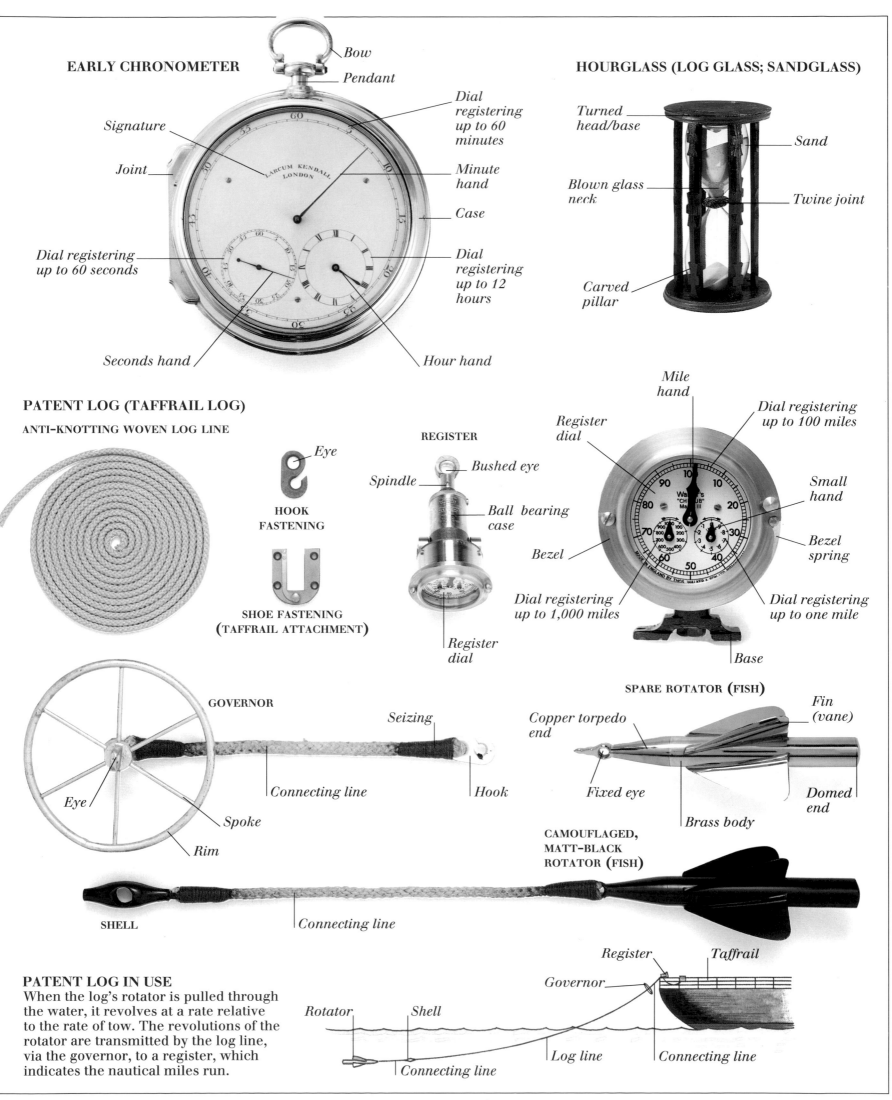

EARLY CHRONOMETER

Bow

Pendant

Signature

Joint

Dial registering up to 60 minutes

Minute hand

Case

Dial registering up to 60 seconds

Dial registering up to 12 hours

Seconds hand

Hour hand

HOURGLASS (LOG GLASS; SANDGLASS)

Turned head/base

Sand

Blown glass neck

Twine joint

Carved pillar

PATENT LOG (TAFFRAIL LOG)

ANTI-KNOTTING WOVEN LOG LINE

Eye

HOOK FASTENING

**SHOE FASTENING
(TAFFRAIL ATTACHMENT)**

REGISTER

Spindle

Bushed eye

Ball bearing case

Register dial

Mile hand

Register dial

Dial registering up to 100 miles

Small hand

Bezel

Bezel spring

Dial registering up to 1,000 miles

Dial registering up to one mile

Base

GOVERNOR

Seizing

Connecting line

Hook

Eye

Spoke

Rim

SPARE ROTATOR (FISH)

Copper torpedo end

Fin (vane)

Fixed eye

Domed end

Brass body

CAMOUFLAGED, MATT-BLACK ROTATOR (FISH)

SHELL

Connecting line

PATENT LOG IN USE
When the log's rotator is pulled through the water, it revolves at a rate relative to the rate of tow. The revolutions of the rotator are transmitted by the log line, via the governor, to a register, which indicates the nautical miles run.

Register

Taffrail

Governor

Rotator

Shell

Log line

Connecting line

Connecting line

Pilotage

NAVIGATING A SHIP from known landmarks close to land or in harbour is known as pilotage. Mariners have a selection of aids, such as the magnetic compass and lead line, to which they can turn to ensure that they are on a safe course. The magnetic compass is based on the attraction of a magnet to magnetic north. A round compass card rests on a pivot, held steady by magnetism; it is marked with 360 degrees or a series of directional "points". These indicate the ship's course. The compass is often housed in a binnacle, a wooden case with correctors that counter the magnetic distortion of an iron ship. Most vessels now use electronic devices to find water depth, but some still use the lead line, marked in fathoms. Terms such as "and a half one" indicate fractions of a fathom. Buoys are floating marks that indicate dangers to navigation, as well as the edges of safe channels. The shape, colour, and top-mark of the buoy indicate its purpose. Lighthouses display a light that flashes in a regular sequence. This sequence is indicated on nautical charts.

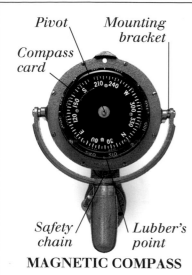

MAGNETIC COMPASS

Pivot
Mounting bracket
Compass card
Safety chain
Lubber's point

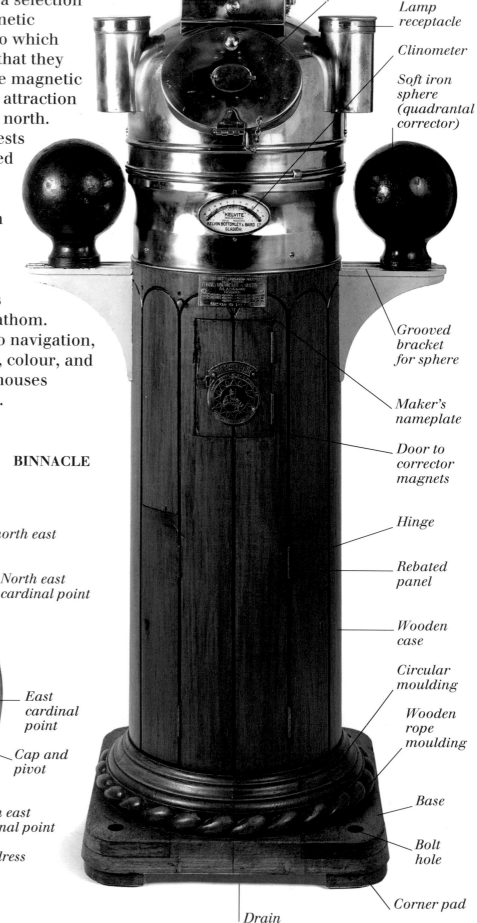

BINNACLE

Hood (cowl)
Shutter covering compass card
Lamp receptacle
Clinometer
Soft iron sphere (quadrantal corrector)
Grooved bracket for sphere
Maker's nameplate
Door to corrector magnets
Hinge
Rebated panel
Wooden case
Circular moulding
Wooden rope moulding
Base
Bolt hole
Corner pad
Drain

18TH CENTURY COMPASS

North cardinal point
Date of manufacture
North north east mark
North east cardinal point
North west cardinal point
Compass card
West cardinal point
East cardinal point
Compass bowl
Cap and pivot
South east cardinal point
South west cardinal point
Maker's address
South cardinal point
Degrees notation
Lubber's point

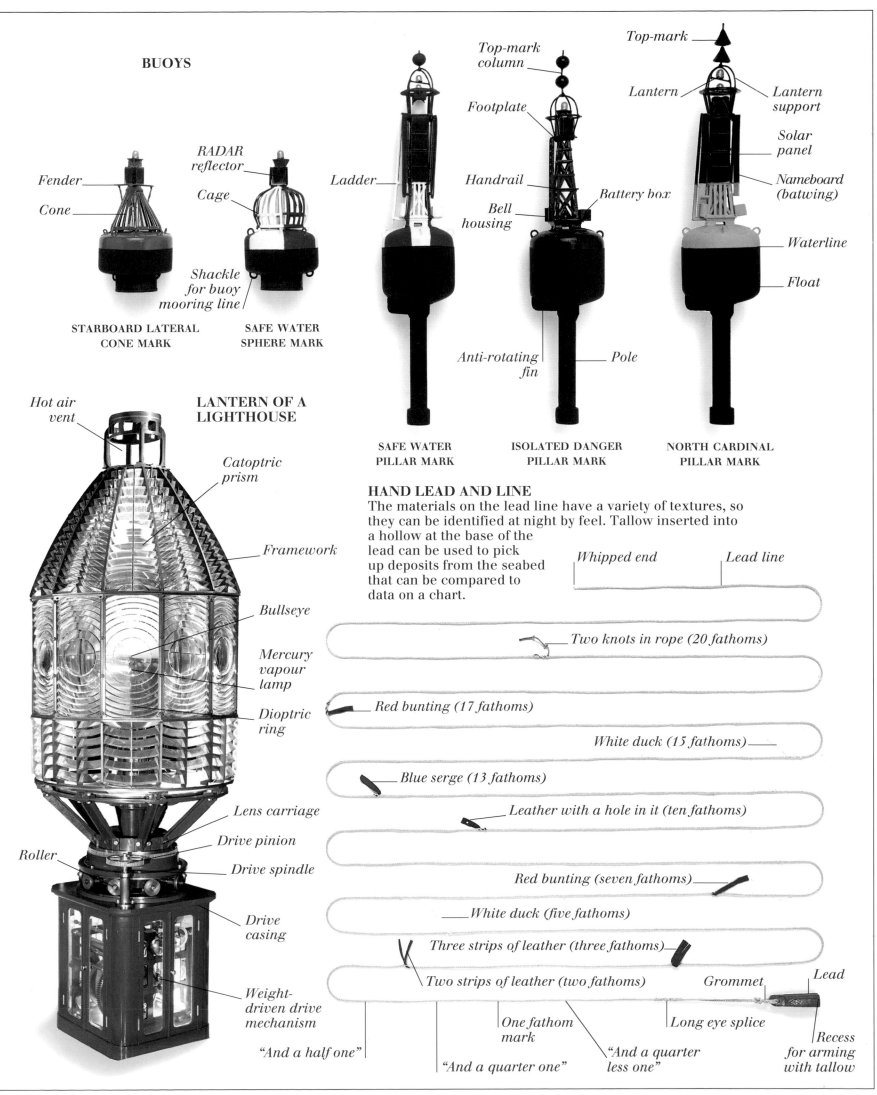

BUOYS

Fender

Cone

RADAR reflector

Cage

Shackle for buoy mooring line

STARBOARD LATERAL CONE MARK

SAFE WATER SPHERE MARK

Top-mark column

Footplate

Ladder

Handrail

Bell housing

Battery box

Anti-rotating fin

Pole

SAFE WATER PILLAR MARK

ISOLATED DANGER PILLAR MARK

Top-mark

Lantern

Lantern support

Solar panel

Nameboard (batwing)

Waterline

Float

NORTH CARDINAL PILLAR MARK

LANTERN OF A LIGHTHOUSE

Hot air vent

Catoptric prism

Framework

Bullseye

Mercury vapour lamp

Dioptric ring

Lens carriage

Drive pinion

Roller

Drive spindle

Drive casing

Weight-driven drive mechanism

HAND LEAD AND LINE
The materials on the lead line have a variety of textures, so they can be identified at night by feel. Tallow inserted into a hollow at the base of the lead can be used to pick up deposits from the seabed that can be compared to data on a chart.

Whipped end

Lead line

Two knots in rope (20 fathoms)

Red bunting (17 fathoms)

White duck (15 fathoms)

Blue serge (13 fathoms)

Leather with a hole in it (ten fathoms)

Red bunting (seven fathoms)

White duck (five fathoms)

Three strips of leather (three fathoms)

Two strips of leather (two fathoms)

Grommet

Lead

One fathom mark

Long eye splice

"And a half one"

"And a quarter one"

"And a quarter less one"

Recess for arming with tallow

Chart instruments

EARLY SEAFARERS COULD CALCULATE THEIR LATITUDE by observing the altitude of certain stars identified from a celestial globe. Modern charts show lines of latitude (parallels) – measured in degrees, minutes, and scconds north or south of the equator – and lines of longitude (meridians) – measured east or west from zero longitude at Greenwich. Rhumb lines intersect all meridians at the same angle, and by following them, the navigator can be sure of keeping a constant course. The chart also shows sea depths, coastlines, shore elevations, lights, and other features identifiable from a ship. The parallel ruler and the breton plotter are both used for plotting courses on a chart, while dividers can be used to measure the distance between charted points. The hand-bearing compass has a sight that a navigator lines up with visible objects, so as to get their compass bearings. True north is at the North Pole. Note that magnetic north (to which a compass needle points) is actually in the middle of the Canadian Arctic.

DIVIDERS

Adjusting screw

Point

CELESTIAL GLOBE

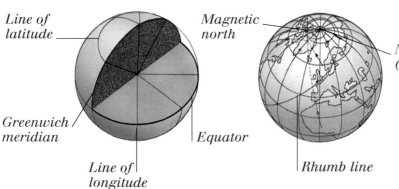

Constellation symbol

Meridian line

Equator

Stand

LATITUDE AND LONGITUDE

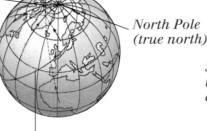

Line of latitude

Greenwich meridian

Equator

Line of longitude

RHUMB LINE

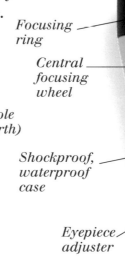

Magnetic north

North Pole (true north)

Rhumb line

BINOCULARS

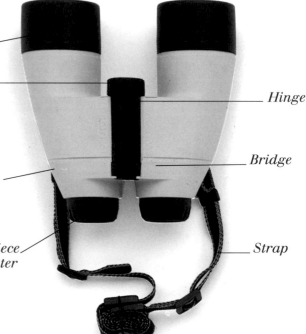

Eyepiece

Focusing ring

Central focusing wheel

Hinge

Shockproof, waterproof case

Bridge

Eyepiece adjuster

Strap

HAND-BEARING COMPASS

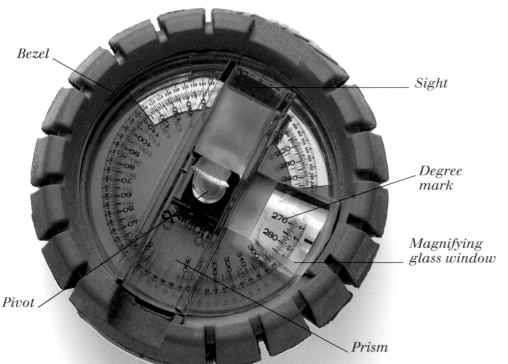

Bezel

Sight

Degree mark

Magnifying glass window

Pivot

Prism

BRETON PLOTTER AND NOTEPAD

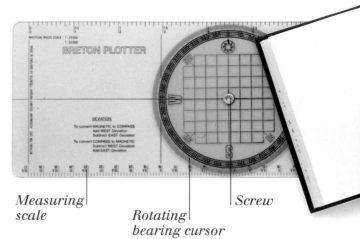

BRETON PLOTTER

Measuring scale

Rotating bearing cursor

Screw

NAUTICAL CHART

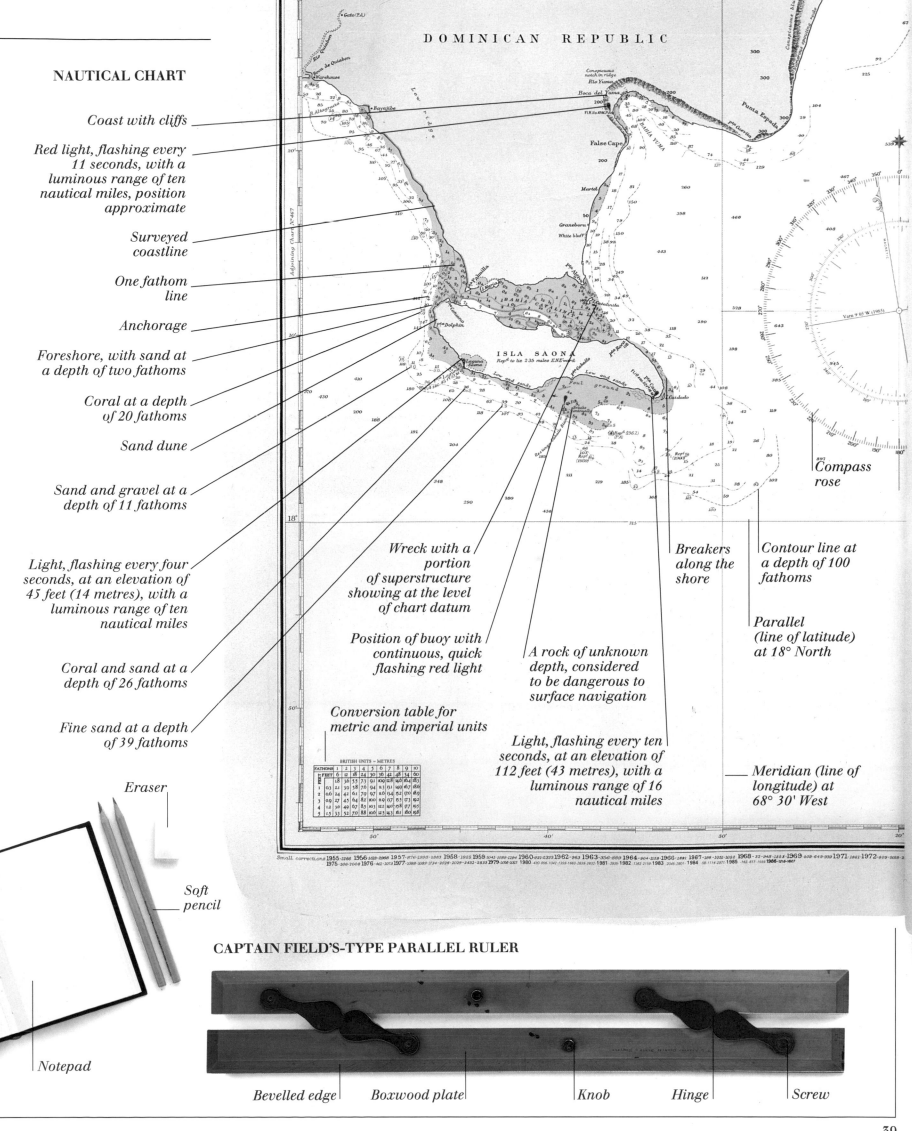

Coast with cliffs

Red light, flashing every 11 seconds, with a luminous range of ten nautical miles, position approximate

Surveyed coastline

One fathom line

Anchorage

Foreshore, with sand at a depth of two fathoms

Coral at a depth of 20 fathoms

Sand dune

Sand and gravel at a depth of 11 fathoms

Light, flashing every four seconds, at an elevation of 45 feet (14 metres), with a luminous range of ten nautical miles

Coral and sand at a depth of 26 fathoms

Fine sand at a depth of 39 fathoms

Eraser

Soft pencil

Notepad

Wreck with a portion of superstructure showing at the level of chart datum

Position of buoy with continuous, quick flashing red light

Conversion table for metric and imperial units

A rock of unknown depth, considered to be dangerous to surface navigation

Light, flashing every ten seconds, at an elevation of 112 feet (43 metres), with a luminous range of 16 nautical miles

Breakers along the shore

Contour line at a depth of 100 fathoms

Parallel (line of latitude) at 18° North

Meridian (line of longitude) at 68° 30' West

Compass rose

CAPTAIN FIELD'S-TYPE PARALLEL RULER

Bevelled edge   Boxwood plate   Knob   Hinge   Screw

Flags

FOR MANY CENTURIES, FLAGS HAVE BEEN USED ON SHIPS to identify themselves, and to pass messages from one ship to another – either friend or foe! Each flag has a basic meaning, which can be changed by hoisting the flag on a different mast, or by hoisting certain combinations of flags. Communication by flag is still very important to ships today; ensigns identify the ship's country of origin, and standardized alphabet and number flags can be used to spell out messages. The flag of the country whose waters a ship is entering must be flown as a matter of courtesy. To save time, solo flags can be used to convey specific messages, as on the page opposite. Other flag systems can be used for specific purposes. For example, semaphore code provides a quick means of sending messages over short distances.

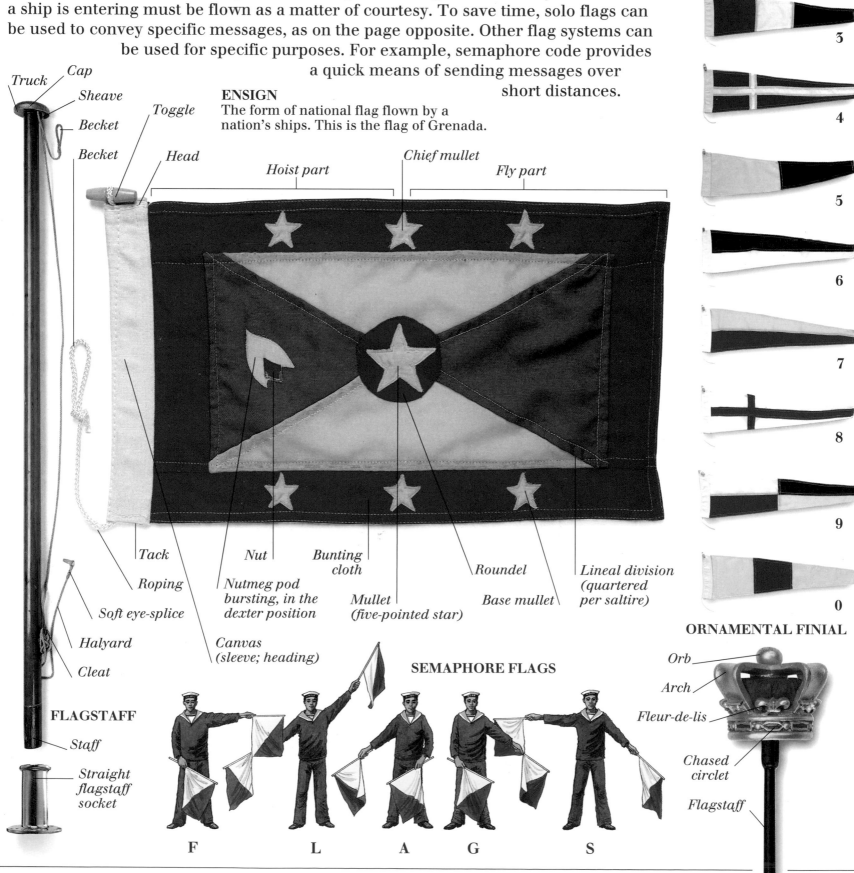

ENSIGN
The form of national flag flown by a nation's ships. This is the flag of Grenada.

Truck
Cap
Sheave
Becket
Toggle
Becket
Head
Hoist part
Chief mullet
Fly part
Tack
Nut
Bunting cloth
Roundel
Lineal division (quartered per saltire)
Roping
Nutmeg pod bursting, in the dexter position
Mullet (five-pointed star)
Base mullet
Soft eye-splice
Canvas (sleeve; heading)
Halyard
Cleat

FLAGSTAFF
Staff
Straight flagstaff socket

SEMAPHORE FLAGS

F   L   A   G   S

1
2
3
4
5
6
7
8
9
0

ORNAMENTAL FINIAL
Orb
Arch
Fleur-de-lis
Chased circlet
Flagstaff

A KEEP WELL CLEAR
AT LOW SPEED

B I AM CARRYING
DANGEROUS GOODS

C YES (AFFIRMATIVE)

D I AM MANOEUVRING
WITH DIFFICULTY

E I AM DIRECTING MY
COURSE TO STARBOARD

F I AM DISABLED;
COMMUNICATE WITH ME

Command flag

Command flag

Ensign

Royal personal
standard

Pennant

Personal
standard

Personal
standard

A DRESSED SHIP SHOWING FLAG POSITIONS

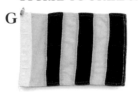

G I REQUIRE A PILOT

H I HAVE A PILOT
ON BOARD

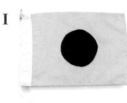

I I AM DIRECTING MY
COURSE TO PORT

J I AM ON FIRE; KEEP
CLEAR OF ME

K I HAVE SOMETHING
TO COMMUNICATE

L YOU SHOULD STOP
YOUR VESSEL

M MY VESSEL IS STOPPED

N NO (NEGATIVE)

O MAN OVERBOARD

P ALL PERSONS TO
REPORT ON BOARD

Q I REQUEST FREE
PRATIQUE

R NO MEANING

S MY ENGINES ARE GOING
FULL SPEED ASTERN

T KEEP CLEAR OF ME

U YOU ARE RUNNING
INTO DANGER

V I REQUIRE ASSISTANCE

W I REQUIRE MEDICAL
ASSISTANCE

X STOP CARRYING OUT
YOUR INTENTIONS

Y I AM DRAGGING
MY ANCHOR

Z I REQUIRE A TUG

ANSWERING PENNANT

FIRST
SUBSTITUTE

SECOND
SUBSTITUTE

THIRD
SUBSTITUTE

Signals

LIKE FLAGS, SOUND AND LIGHT SIGNALS are used to warn other vessels of a ship's movements. Signalling systems overlap and are complementary to each other. A Very pistol was used to fire pyrotechnic lights of various colours and patterns. These patterns conveyed messages to other craft or to the shore. Today the Very pistol is sometimes used to fire distress signals. Morse code is based on combinations of dots and dashes of sound or light that can be used to send messages. The interval of one dash is equal to three dots. The Aldis lamp sends messages in morse code by means of a shutter-trigger-operated mirror. Piping on a boatswain's call is another way of passing orders and information. Navigation lights identify the port and starboard sides of a ship at night. In poor visibility, the foghorn must be sounded. Combinations of short or long blasts convey particular meanings. When helping small craft to come alongside the parent ship, the quartermaster uses the code of hand signals shown opposite. The ship's bell is used primarily to signal the time.

Crown
Wire
Engraved lettering
MAURETANIA
Shoulder
Waist
Wire
Lip
Mouth

SHIP'S BELL
Throughout each four-hour watch, hours and half-hours are struck by a ship's bell. The time can therefore be described as "one bell" for the first half hour, "two bells" for the second half hour, and so on up to eight bells.

Muzzle
Barrel

MORSE CODE

A ●▬	J ●▬▬▬	R ●▬●
B ▬●●●	K ▬●▬	S ●●●
C ▬●▬●	L ●▬●●	T ▬
D ▬●●	M ▬▬	U ●●▬
E ●	N ▬●	V ●●●▬
F ●●▬●	O ▬▬▬	W ●▬▬
G ▬▬●	P ●▬▬●	X ▬●●▬
H ●●●●	Q ▬▬●▬	Y ▬●▬▬
I ●●		Z ▬▬●●

ALDIS LAMP
This Aldis lamp has been partially dismantled to show the reflector housing.

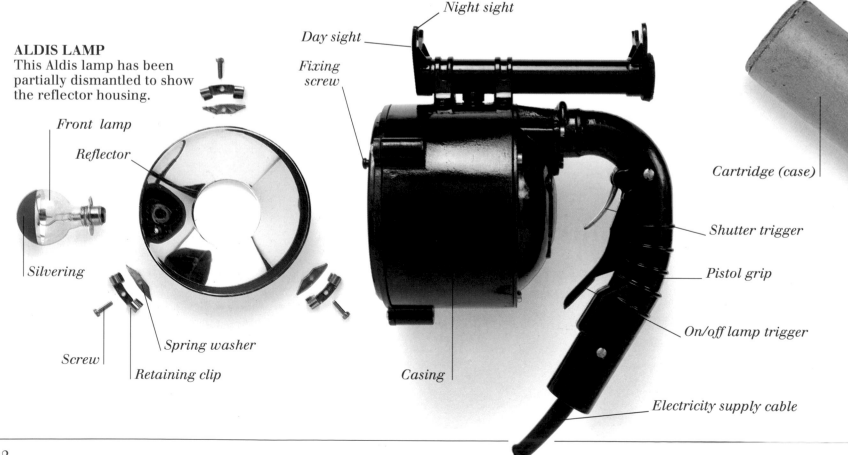

Night sight
Day sight
Fixing screw

Front lamp
Reflector
Silvering
Screw
Spring washer
Retaining clip
Casing

Cartridge (case)
Shutter trigger
Pistol grip
On/off lamp trigger
Electricity supply cable

VERY PISTOL (SIGNALLING PISTOL)

Flashguard (lug)

Chamber

Extractor

Extractor pin

Stirrup

Hammer

Stirrup fastening screw

WEBLEY & SCOTT LTD LONDON & BIRMINGHAM

Joint axis pin

Body (frame)

Hammer screw

Pistol mark

Maker's name

Trigger

Year of acceptance into ship's store

Trigger guard

Government inspector's mark

Trigger screw

Stock screw

Stock (grip)

Rim

Butt

Metal sleeve (head)

Butt swivel (butt lanyard ring)

FOGHORN

Pipe

Button

Bell

Dioptric lens

Port side lens

Starboard side lens

Gas bottle

Spiral tungsten halogen bulb

Base

NAVIGATION LIGHT

Gun

Buoy

Inscription

Hole

Mouthpiece

Shackle

Keel

BOATSWAIN'S CALL
This whistle has two main notes – a "low" and a "high" – and three tones – a "plain", a "warble", and a "trill".

GANGWAY HAND SIGNALS

CARRY ON

LIE OFF

Boatswain's call

MAKE FAST

COME ALONGSIDE

Gangway

The liferaft

IT IS CRUCIAL THAT ALL VESSELS are equipped with the lifesaving gear appropriate to their sailing conditions. The liferaft shown is intended to hold four people in the roughest seas. It is designed to maintain body heat, stay afloat, avoid capsizing, and inflate quickly. It should be tethered to the ship by a painter. In an emergency the crew throw the liferaft overboard and tug on the painter, which releases carbon dioxide from a pressurized cylinder and inflates the raft. Once aboard, the crew sever the painter, release the drogue (sea anchor), examine their emergency pack, and hope that they soon sight land or another ship.

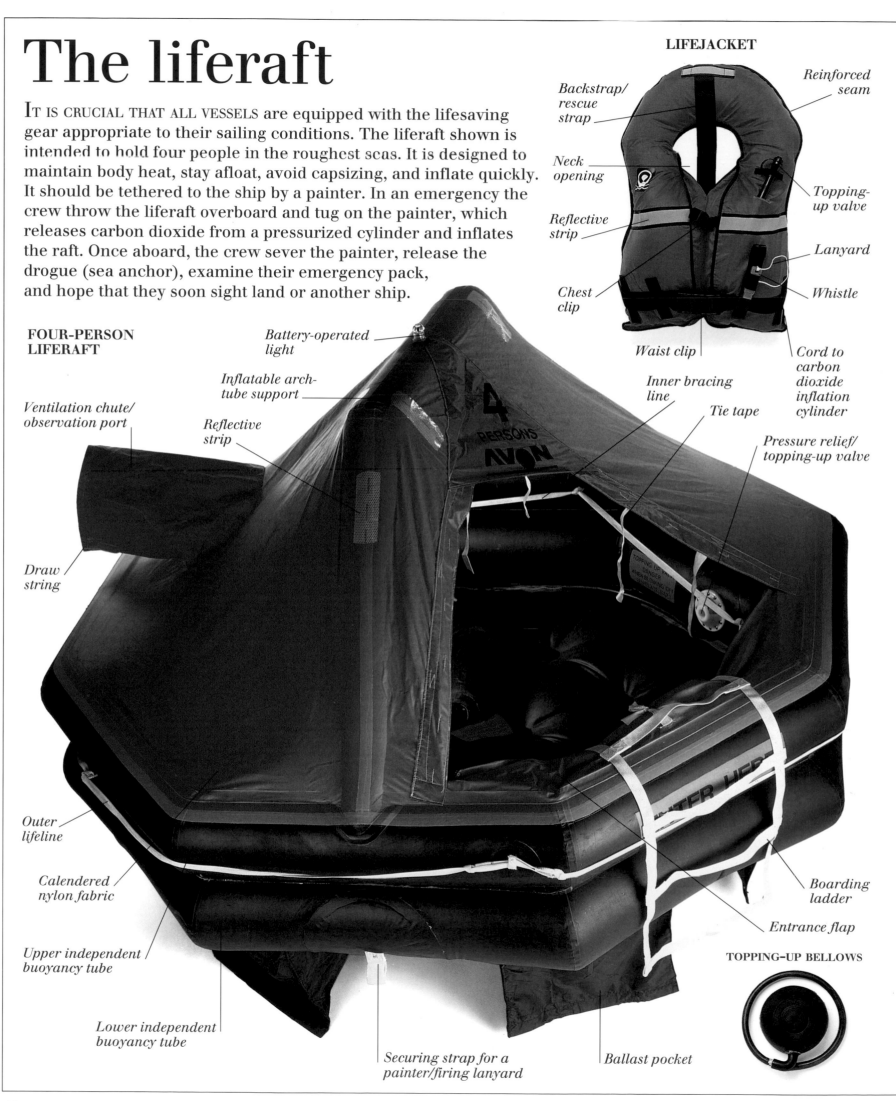

LIFEJACKET

Backstrap/ rescue strap

Reinforced seam

Neck opening

Topping- up valve

Reflective strip

Lanyard

Chest clip

Whistle

Waist clip

Cord to carbon dioxide inflation cylinder

FOUR-PERSON LIFERAFT

Battery-operated light

Inflatable arch- tube support

Ventilation chute/ observation port

Reflective strip

Inner bracing line

Tie tape

Pressure relief/ topping-up valve

Draw string

Outer lifeline

Calendered nylon fabric

Boarding ladder

Entrance flap

Upper independent buoyancy tube

TOPPING-UP BELLOWS

Lower independent buoyancy tube

Securing strap for a painter/firing lanyard

Ballast pocket

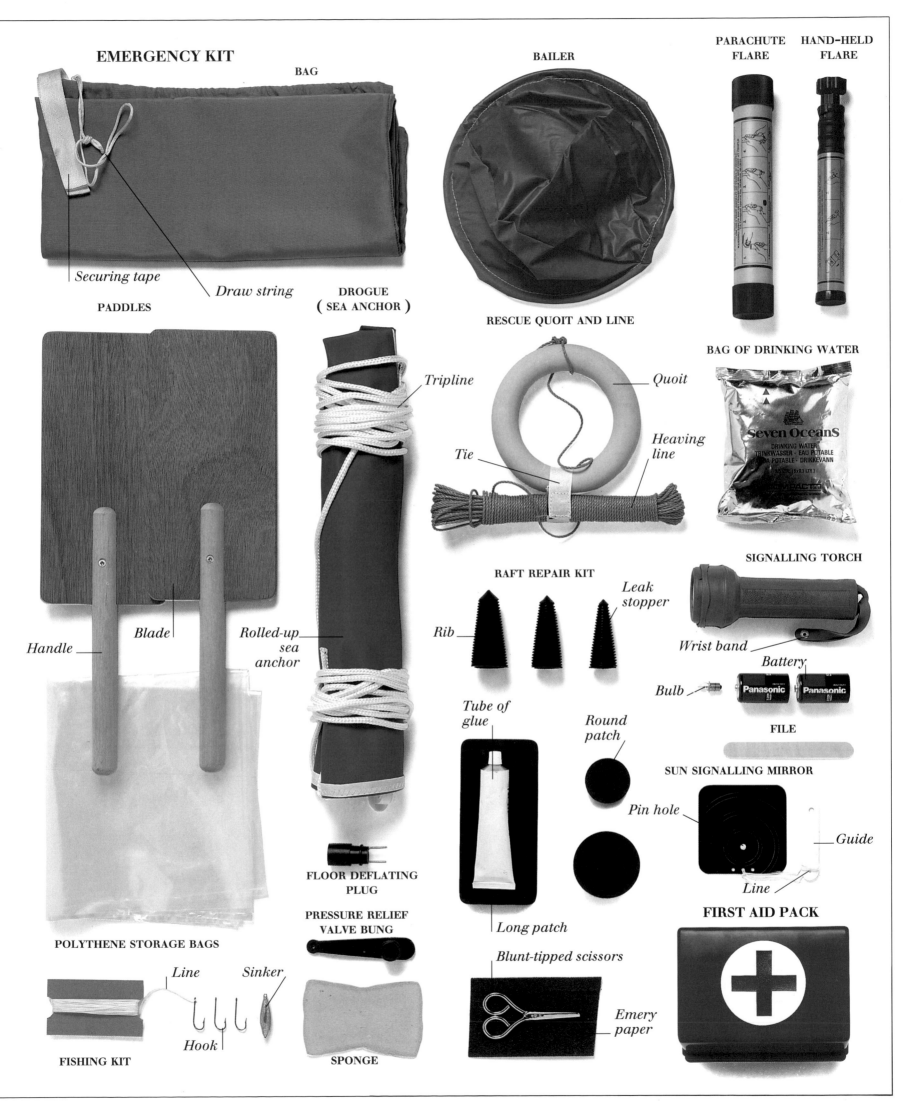

EMERGENCY KIT

BAG

BAILER

PARACHUTE
FLARE

HAND–HELD
FLARE

Securing tape

Draw string

PADDLES

DROGUE
(SEA ANCHOR)

RESCUE QUOIT AND LINE

Tripline

Quoit

Tie

*Heaving
line*

BAG OF DRINKING WATER

Seven OceanS
DRINKING WATER
TRINKWASSER · EAU POTABLE
AGUA POTABLE · DRIKKEVANN

SIGNALLING TORCH

RAFT REPAIR KIT

*Leak
stopper*

Blade

*Rolled-up
sea
anchor*

Rib

Wrist band

Handle

Battery

Bulb

Panasonic   Panasonic

FILE

*Tube of
glue*

*Round
patch*

SUN SIGNALLING MIRROR

Pin hole

Guide

FLOOR DEFLATING
PLUG

Line

POLYTHENE STORAGE BAGS

PRESSURE RELIEF
VALVE BUNG

Long patch

FIRST AID PACK

Line   *Sinker*

Blunt-tipped scissors

Hook

*Emery
paper*

FISHING KIT

SPONGE

Mooring and anchoring

FOR LARGE VESSELS IN OPEN WATER, ANCHORAGE IS ESSENTIAL. By holding a ship securely to the seabed, an anchor prevents the vessel from being at the mercy of wave, tide, and current. The earliest anchors were nothing more than stones. In later years, many anchors had a standard design, much like the Admiralty pattern anchor shown on this page. The Danforth anchor is somewhat different. It has particularly deep flukes to give it great holding power. On large sailing ships, anchors were worked by teams of sailors. They turned the drum of a capstan by pushing on bars slotted into the revolving cylinder. This, in turn, lifted or lowered the anchor chain. In calm harbours and estuaries, ships can moor (make fast) without using anchors. Berthing ropes can be attached to bollards both inboard and on the quayside. Berthing ropes are joined to each other by bends, like those opposite.

STONE ANCHOR (KILLICK)

Rope hole

TYPES OF ANCHOR

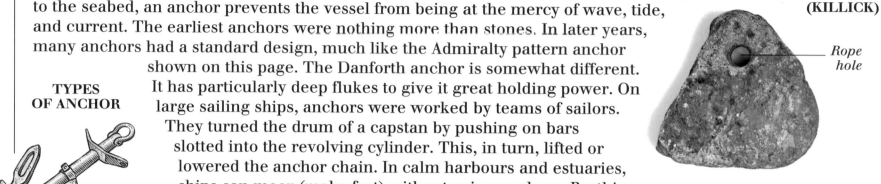

CLOSE-STOWING ANCHOR

CQR ANCHOR (SECURE ANCHOR; PLOUGH ANCHOR)

ADMIRALTY ANCHOR TYPE ACII

ADMIRALTY PATTERN ANCHOR

STOCKLESS ANCHOR

MUSHROOM ANCHOR (PERMANENT MOORING ANCHOR)

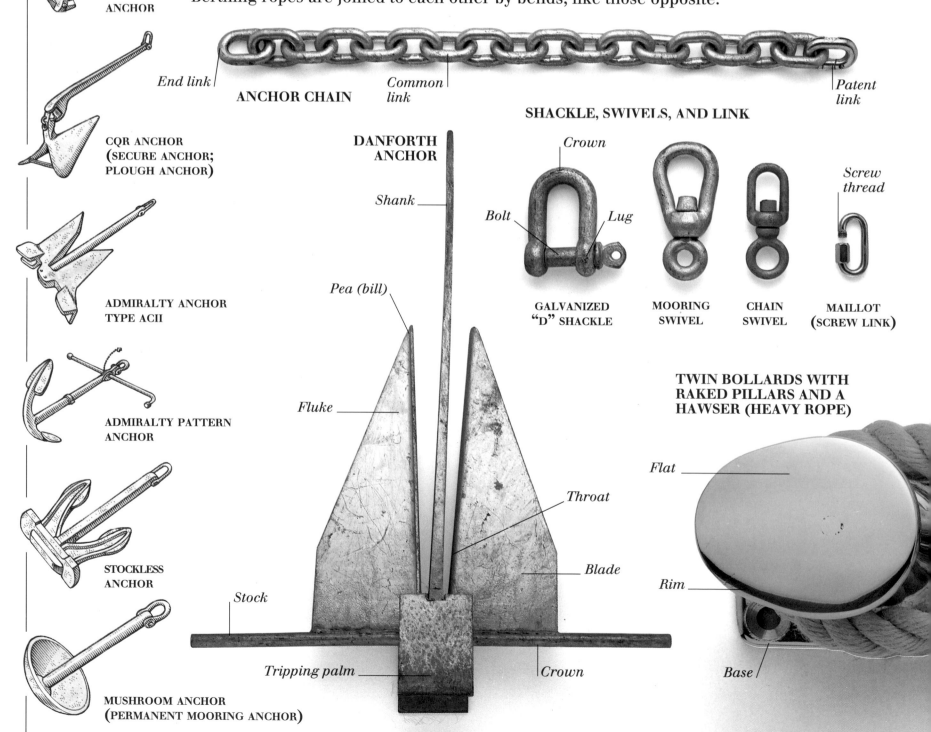

End link

ANCHOR CHAIN

Common link

Patent link

SHACKLE, SWIVELS, AND LINK

DANFORTH ANCHOR

Crown

Shank

Bolt

Lug

Screw thread

Pea (bill)

Fluke

GALVANIZED "D" SHACKLE

MOORING SWIVEL

CHAIN SWIVEL

MAILLOT (SCREW LINK)

Throat

TWIN BOLLARDS WITH RAKED PILLARS AND A HAWSER (HEAVY ROPE)

Flat

Blade

Rim

Stock

Tripping palm

Crown

Base

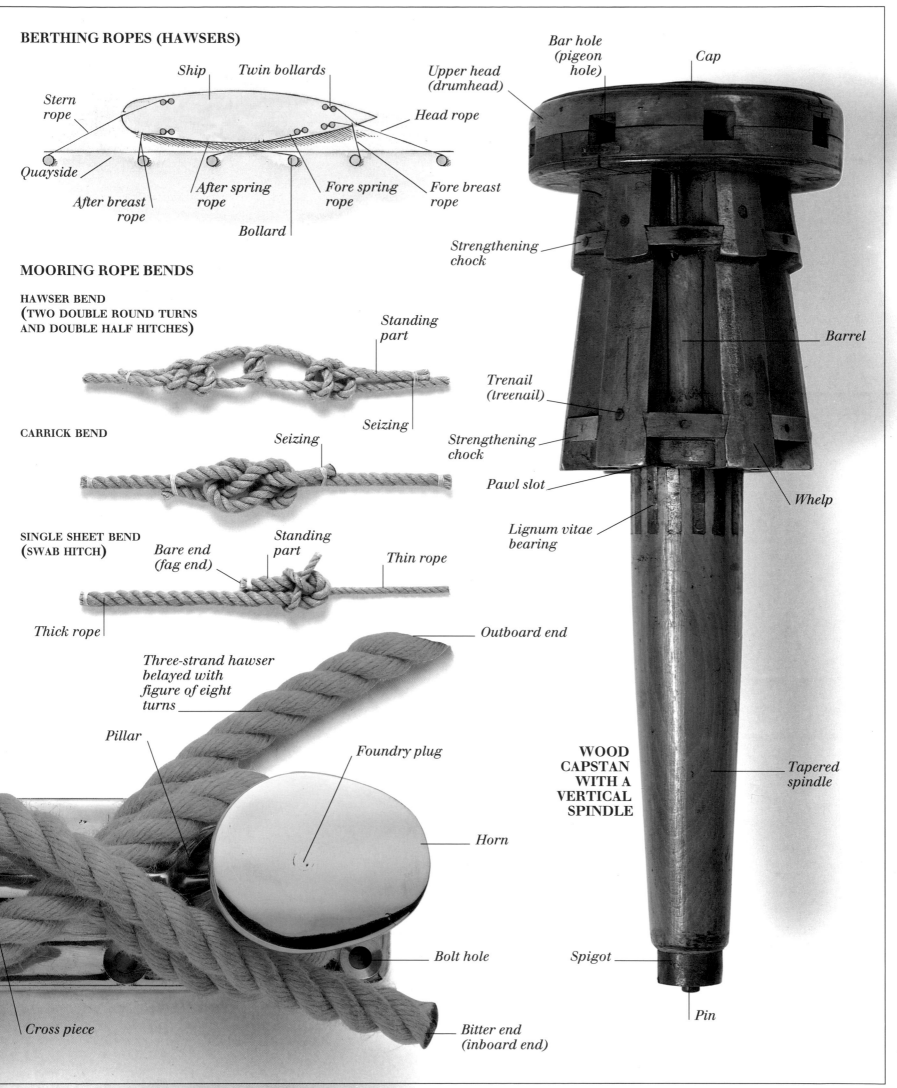

BERTHING ROPES (HAWSERS)

Ship
Twin bollards
Stern rope
Upper head (drumhead)
Bar hole (pigeon hole)
Cap
Head rope
Quayside
After spring rope
Fore spring rope
Fore breast rope
After breast rope
Bollard
Strengthening chock

MOORING ROPE BENDS

HAWSER BEND
(TWO DOUBLE ROUND TURNS
AND DOUBLE HALF HITCHES)

Standing part

Barrel

Seizing

CARRICK BEND

Trenail (treenail)

Seizing

Strengthening chock

SINGLE SHEET BEND
(SWAB HITCH)

Standing part
Bare end (fag end)
Thin rope
Thick rope

Pawl slot

Whelp

Lignum vitae bearing

Outboard end

Three-strand hawser belayed with figure of eight turns

Pillar

Foundry plug

WOOD CAPSTAN WITH A VERTICAL SPINDLE

Tapered spindle

Horn

Bolt hole

Spigot

Pin

Cross piece

Bitter end (inboard end)

Ropes and knots

ALL KINDS OF ROPES ARE USED AT SEA, from thin twines and yarns to thick hawsers. Synthetic fibres have been developed specifically for use at sea. Nylon ropes stretch, and so are ideal for anchoring; polypropylene has little stretch, so is ideal for halyards and sheets. Different types of knots are used for different purposes. Knots that join two ropes are called bends; hitches join a rope to another object; and bowlines produce an eye (loop) in the end of a rope. Ropes can be joined by splicing (unravelling the ends and weaving them together) or seizing (lashing the ropes together side by side).

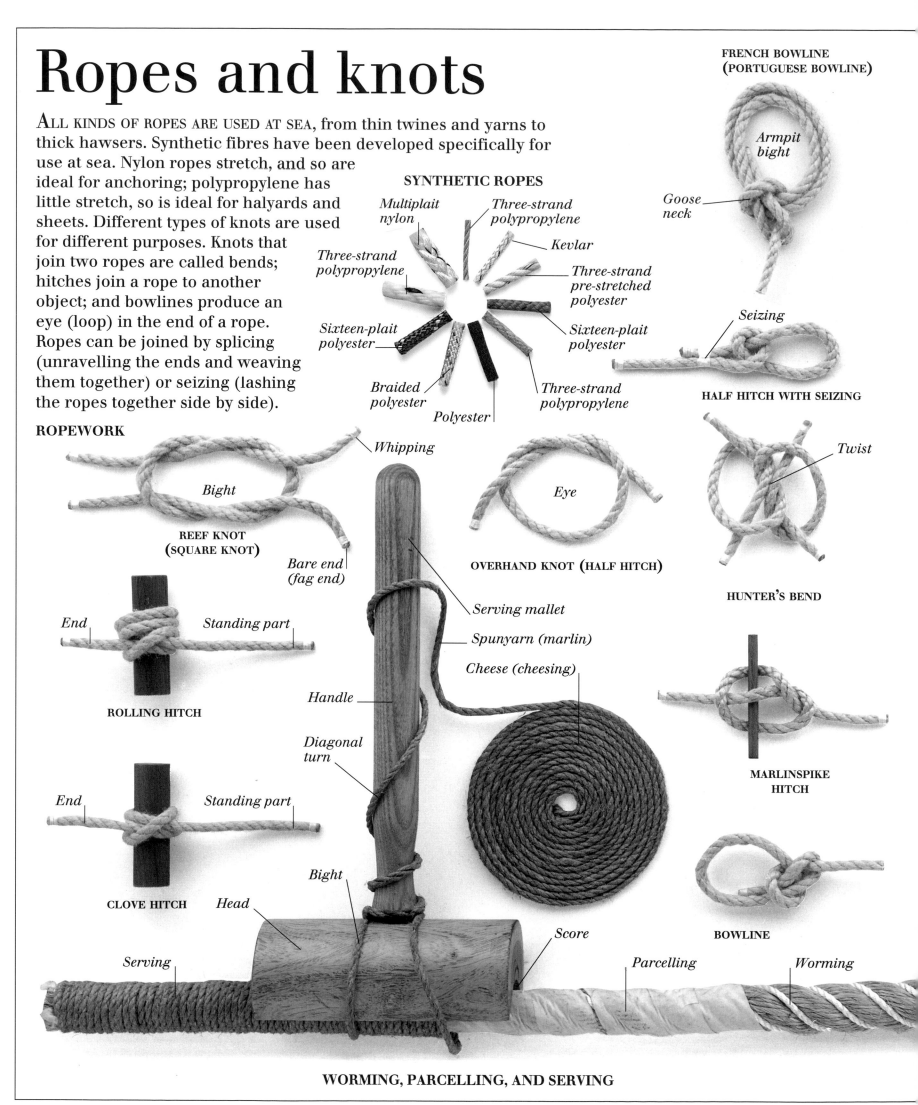

FRENCH BOWLINE (PORTUGUESE BOWLINE)

Armpit bight

Goose neck

SYNTHETIC ROPES

Multiplait nylon

Three-strand polypropylene

Three-strand polypropylene

Kevlar

Three-strand pre-stretched polyester

Sixteen-plait polyester

Sixteen-plait polyester

Braided polyester

Polyester

Three-strand polypropylene

Seizing

HALF HITCH WITH SEIZING

ROPEWORK

Whipping

Bight

REEF KNOT (SQUARE KNOT)

Bare end (fag end)

Serving mallet

Spunyarn (marlin)

Cheese (cheesing)

Eye

OVERHAND KNOT (HALF HITCH)

Twist

HUNTER'S BEND

End

Standing part

ROLLING HITCH

Handle

Diagonal turn

MARLINSPIKE HITCH

End

Standing part

CLOVE HITCH

Head

Bight

Score

BOWLINE

Serving

Parcelling

Worming

WORMING, PARCELLING, AND SERVING

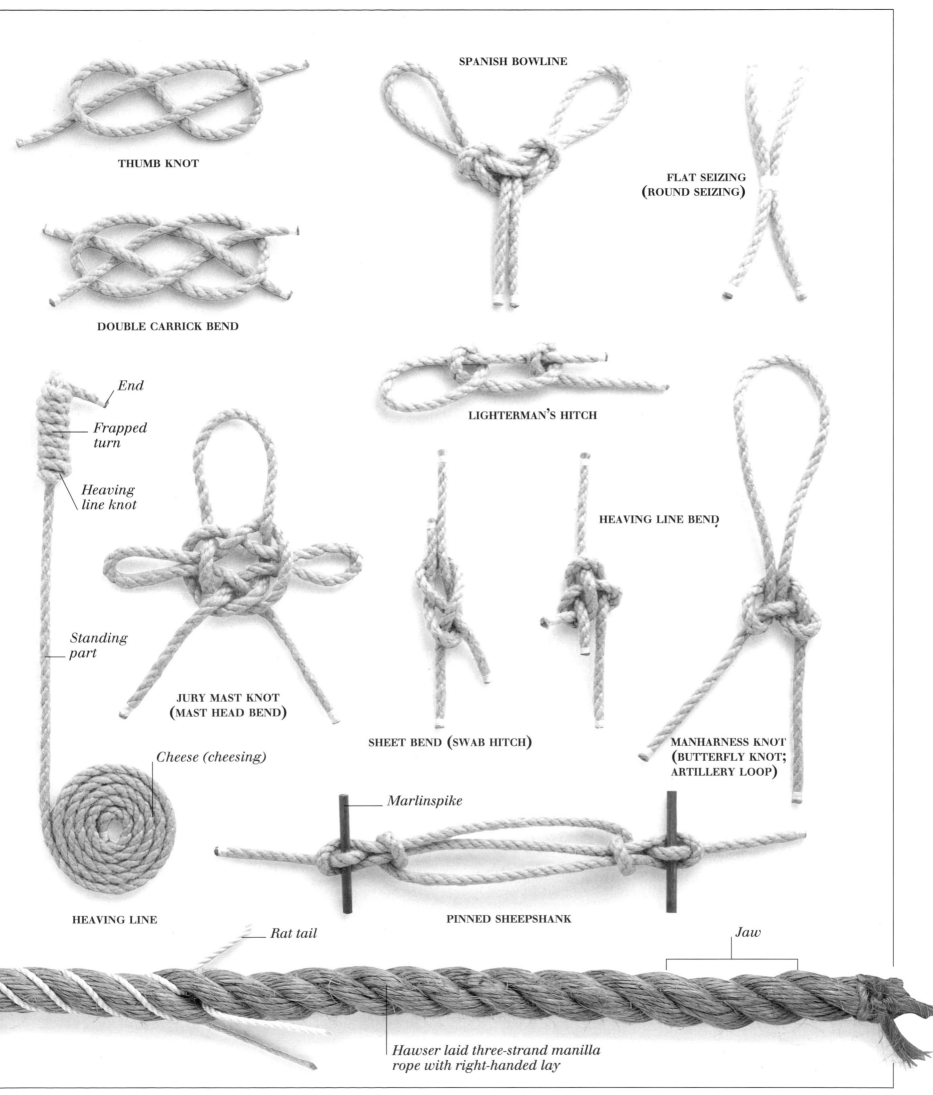

THUMB KNOT

SPANISH BOWLINE

FLAT SEIZING (ROUND SEIZING)

DOUBLE CARRICK BEND

End

Frapped turn

Heaving line knot

LIGHTERMAN'S HITCH

HEAVING LINE BEND

Standing part

JURY MAST KNOT (MAST HEAD BEND)

SHEET BEND (SWAB HITCH)

MANHARNESS KNOT (BUTTERFLY KNOT; ARTILLERY LOOP)

Cheese (cheesing)

Marlinspike

HEAVING LINE

PINNED SHEEPSHANK

Jaw

Rat tail

Hawser laid three-strand manilla rope with right-handed lay

49

Sailing clothing

THE PRINCIPAL FUNCTIONS OF SAILING CLOTHING are to maintain body temperature, be waterproof, and allow freedom of movement. The clothing shown is intended for long distance and foul weather sailing. Water and wind both contribute to loss of body heat, and modern sailing clothing protects the body efficiently by allowing the formation of a layer of warm air around the body. The materials used must be lightweight and quick-drying. This jacket has numerous safety features, including lifejacket, safety harness, whistle, and a pocket for emergency flares.

OLD-FASHIONED LIFEJACKETS
Early lifejackets were made of cork, or silky fibres known as kapok.

Cork lifejacket

Kapok lifejacket

Oilskin

Sou'wester

GLOVE

Water-resistant leather palm

Removable lining

Anti-seasickness wrist band

Adjustable storm cuff

High-intensity strobe light

Carabiner (double-action safety hook)

Lifejacket pull tag

Nylon safety line

OCEAN-SAILING TROUSERS

Braces

Webbing

Chest-high handwarmer pocket

ACCESSORIES

Heavy-duty zip

Thigh pocket

Nylon reinforcement

HAND WARMER

Metal casing

Charcoal

Zinc cream

Applicator

SUN PROTECTION

KNIFE AND SHEATH

Handle

SHACKLE PIN

Eye

Point

Sheath

Blade

DECK BOOT

DECK SHOES

Oiled leather upper

Rot-proof synthetic thread

Non-slip sole

Watertight adjustable collar

Adjustable ankle fastener

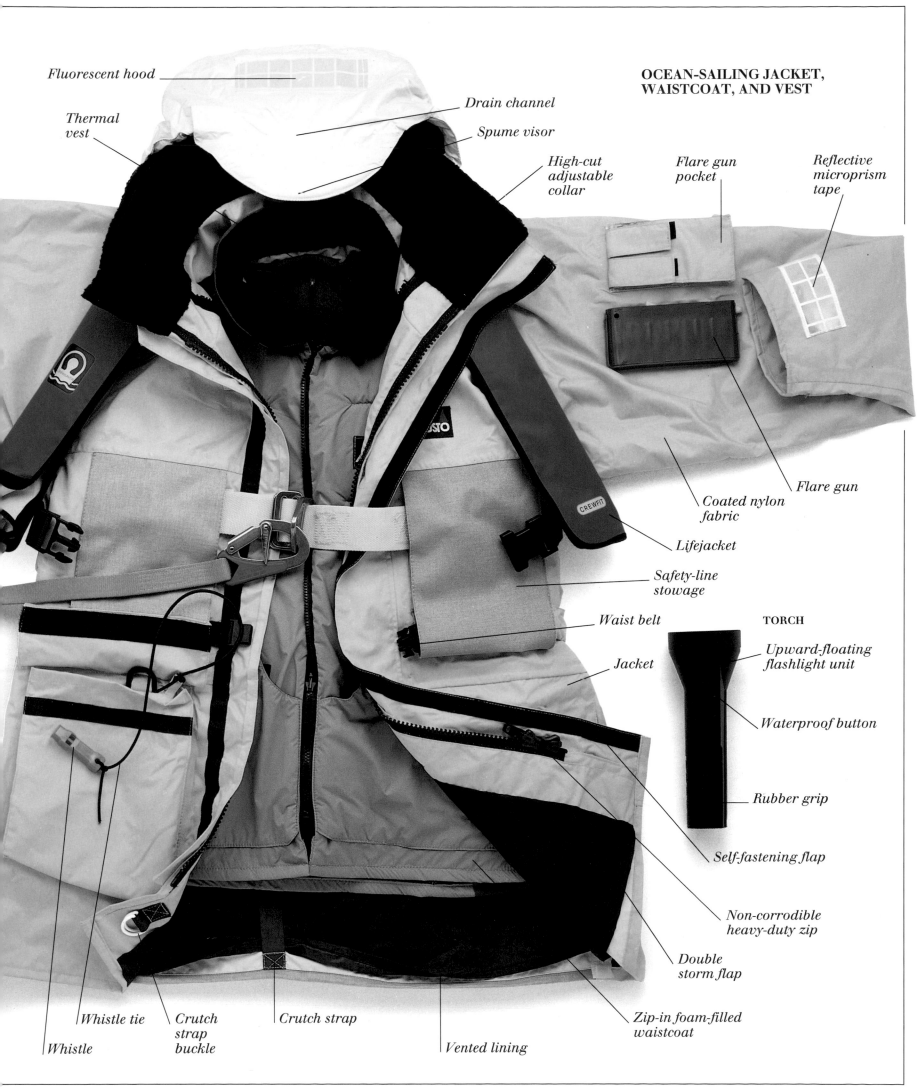

Fluorescent hood

Thermal vest

Drain channel

Spume visor

High-cut adjustable collar

Flare gun pocket

Reflective microprism tape

Coated nylon fabric

Flare gun

Lifejacket

Safety-line stowage

Waist belt

Jacket

TORCH

Upward-floating flashlight unit

Waterproof button

Rubber grip

Self-fastening flap

Non-corrodible heavy-duty zip

Double storm flap

Zip-in foam-filled waistcoat

Whistle tie

Crutch strap buckle

Crutch strap

Whistle

Vented lining

51

The battleship

In the early years of the 20th century, sea warfare – attacking enemy vessels or defending a ship – was revolutionized by the introduction of Dreadnought-type battleships like the Brazilian vessel below. These new ships combined the latest advances in steam propulsion, gunnery, and armour plating. The gun turret was designed to fire shells over huge distances. It was protected by armour 30 cm (12 in) thick. The measurements given for the guns of this ship refer to the bore diameter. Where "weight" is quoted, this is the weight of the shell that the gun fires. Torpedoes – as portrayed on the upper cigarette card (right) – were self-propelled underwater missiles, often steered by gyro-control. Depth charges were designed in the First World War for use against submerged U-boats. They are canisters filled with explosives that are detonated by depth-sensitive pistols. The lower cigarette card shows depth charges being fired by a "thrower", fired from a torpedo tube, and rolled from the stern. Ship's shields were fitted to warships from the late 19th century onwards. The shield shown opposite depicts a traditional ship's cannon.

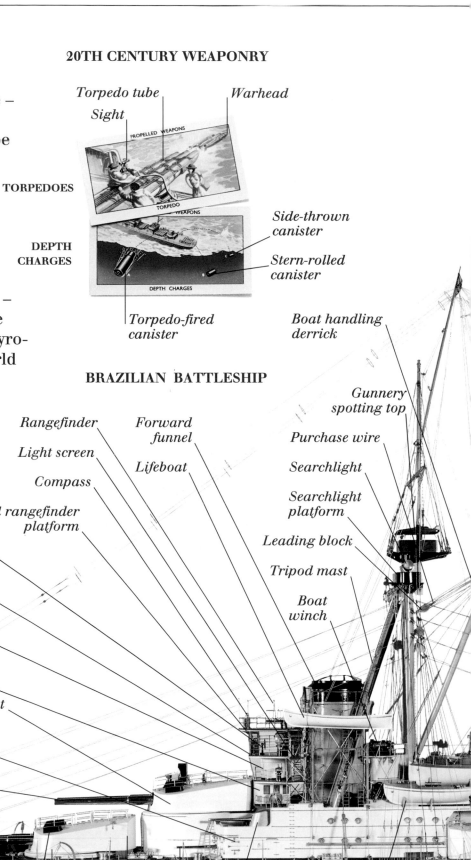

20TH CENTURY WEAPONRY

Torpedo tube

Warhead

Sight

TORPEDOES

Side-thrown canister

DEPTH CHARGES

Stern-rolled canister

Torpedo-fired canister

Boat handling derrick

BRAZILIAN BATTLESHIP

Rangefinder

Forward funnel

Gunnery spotting top

Light screen

Lifeboat

Purchase wire

Compass

Searchlight

Compass and rangefinder platform

Searchlight platform

Ship's wheel

Leading block

Tripod mast

Navigating bridge

Boat winch

Conning tower

Captain's shelter/ chart house

Arms of Brazil

Weather shutter for gun

"F" turret

Jack staff

30 cm (12 in) gun

Skylight

Porthole

Forward accommodation ladder

Sighting hood

"A" turret

Open gun mounting

Steam launch

Stem (false ram bow)

Belt armour

Turret barbette

12 cm (4.7 in) gun

Guest boat boom

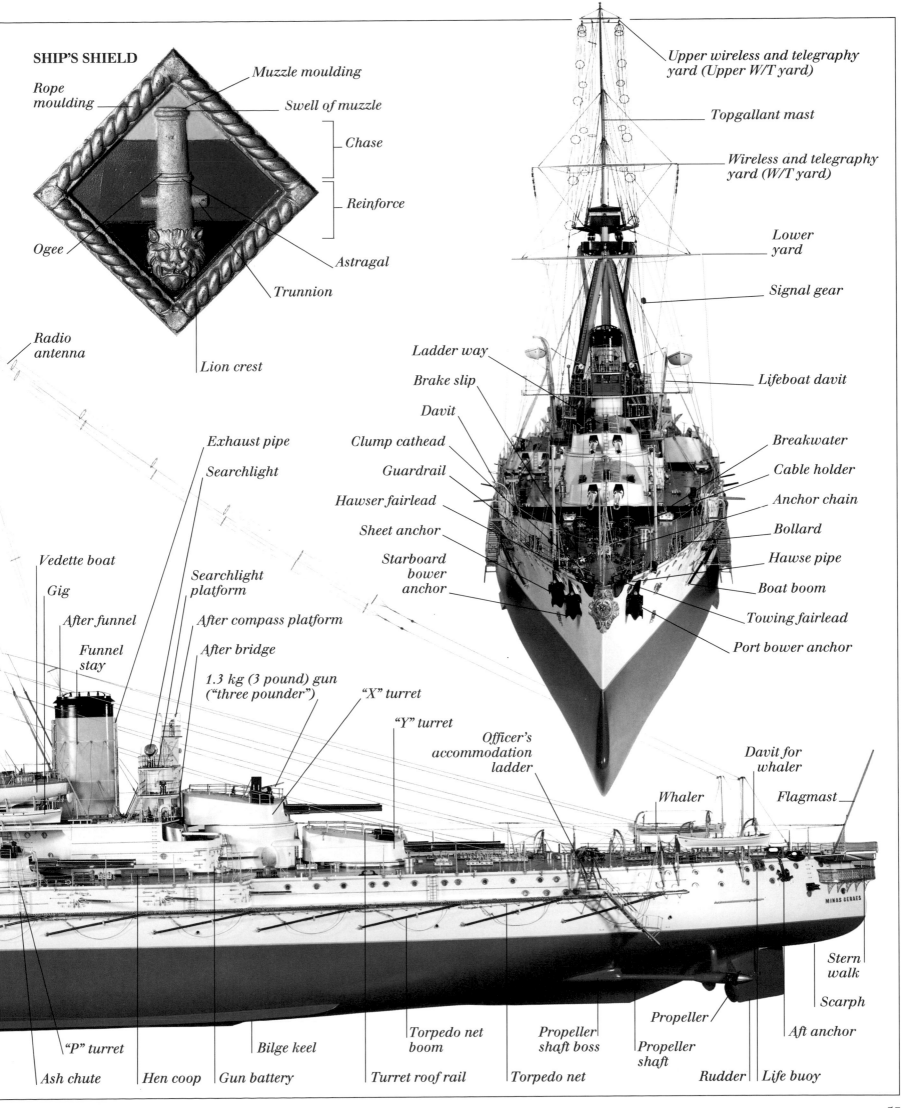

SHIP'S SHIELD

Rope moulding

Muzzle moulding

Swell of muzzle

Chase

Reinforce

Ogee

Astragal

Trunnion

Lion crest

Radio antenna

Upper wireless and telegraphy yard (Upper W/T yard)

Topgallant mast

Wireless and telegraphy yard (W/T yard)

Lower yard

Signal gear

Ladder way

Brake slip

Davit

Clump cathead

Guardrail

Hawser fairlead

Sheet anchor

Starboard bower anchor

Lifeboat davit

Breakwater

Cable holder

Anchor chain

Bollard

Hawse pipe

Boat boom

Towing fairlead

Port bower anchor

Exhaust pipe

Searchlight

Vedette boat

Gig

After funnel

Funnel stay

Searchlight platform

After compass platform

After bridge

1.3 kg (3 pound) gun ("three pounder")

"X" turret

"Y" turret

Officer's accommodation ladder

Davit for whaler

Whaler

Flagmast

Stern walk

Scarph

"P" turret

Bilge keel

Torpedo net boom

Propeller shaft boss

Propeller

Aft anchor

Ash chute

Hen coop

Gun battery

Turret roof rail

Torpedo net

Propeller shaft

Rudder

Life buoy

53

Fighting at sea

FROM THE MID-19TH CENTURY, ARMOURED SHIPS provided a new challenge to enemy craft. In response, huge revolving gun turrets were developed. These could fire in any direction, could be loaded from the breech very rapidly, and, instead of cannonballs, they discharged exploding shells. Modern fighting ships, like the frigate, combine heavy ship-borne armament with light helicopter weaponry. Submarines function below the surface of the sea. Their speed and ability to fire missiles from under water are their major assets. The nuclear submarine can stay under water for several years without refuelling.

Stabilized fin

Aft hydroplane

Propeller

Lower rudder

Rangefinder

Look out periscope

Local control cabinet

Breech wheel

Breech block

Loading arm

Slide locking lever

Slide

Sighting hood

Recoil cylinder

Elevating wheel

Guide for gun loading cage

Rammer lever

Gun loading cage

Blast bag (breeches)

Floor of gun house

Turret roller

Training rack gearing

Roller path

Working chamber

GUN TURRET
In this turret for two 37 cm (15 in) guns, shells are carried in a hoisting cage. The shell is rammed into the gun, followed by the propellant (charge). Once the breech is closed, the gun is ready for firing. The whole operation requires around 70 sailors.

Training gear

Rammer

Waiting position

Roller path support

Floor

"Walking pipe" (water supply)

Barbette (armour)

Main hoisting cage

Turret trunk

Cordite handling room

Cordite supply shuttle

Ensign staff

FRIGATE

Lynx helicopter

SONAR torpedo decoy

Cordite case

Rudder

Practice projectile

High-explosive projectile

Shell bogie

Shell room

Hydraulic grab

Shell-handling gear

Variable pitch propeller

Ladder way

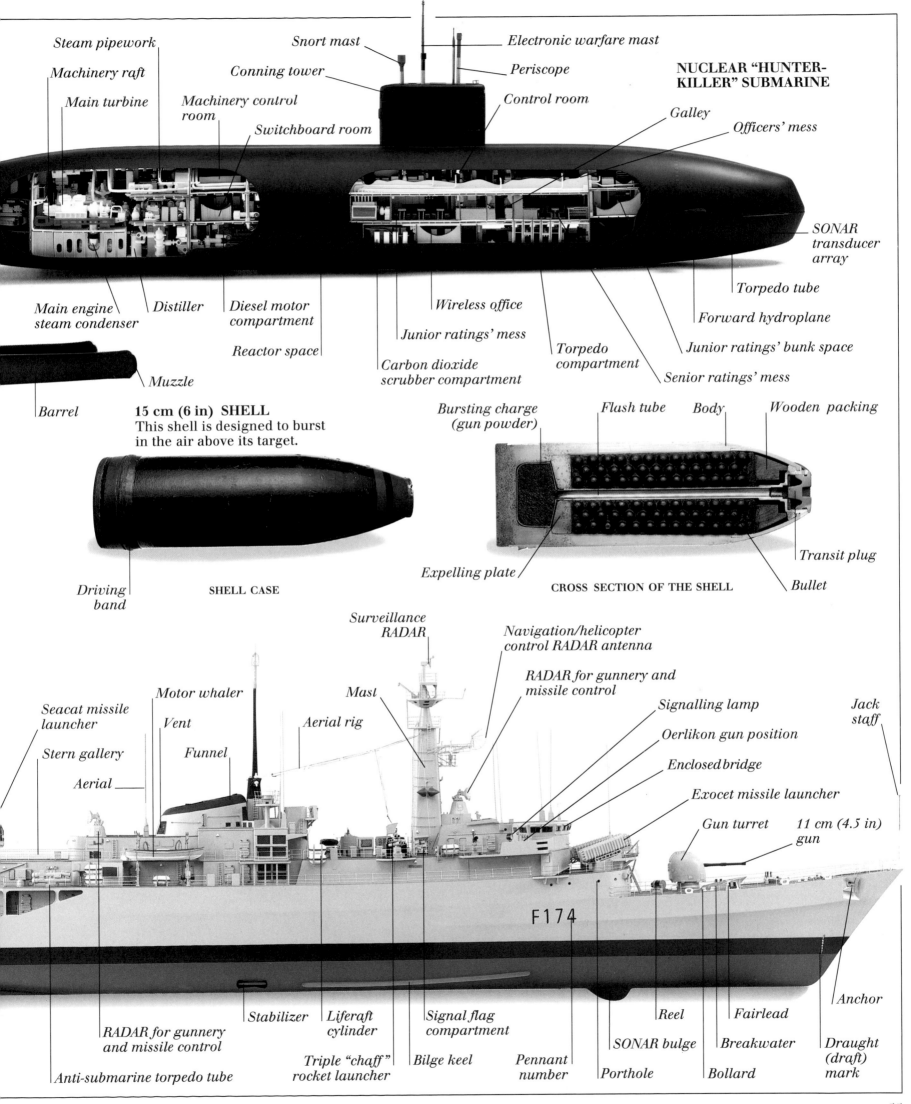

NUCLEAR "HUNTER-KILLER" SUBMARINE

Steam pipework

Machinery raft

Main turbine

Snort mast

Conning tower

Machinery control room

Switchboard room

Electronic warfare mast

Periscope

Control room

Galley

Officers' mess

SONAR transducer array

Main engine steam condenser

Distiller

Diesel motor compartment

Reactor space

Muzzle

Barrel

Wireless office

Junior ratings' mess

Carbon dioxide scrubber compartment

Torpedo compartment

Senior ratings' mess

Torpedo tube

Forward hydroplane

Junior ratings' bunk space

15 cm (6 in) SHELL
This shell is designed to burst in the air above its target.

Bursting charge (gun powder)

Flash tube

Body

Wooden packing

Transit plug

Expelling plate

Bullet

Driving band

SHELL CASE

CROSS SECTION OF THE SHELL

Surveillance RADAR

Navigation/helicopter control RADAR antenna

Motor whaler

Mast

RADAR for gunnery and missile control

Signalling lamp

Jack staff

Seacat missile launcher

Vent

Aerial rig

Oerlikon gun position

Stern gallery

Funnel

Enclosed bridge

Aerial

Exocet missile launcher

Gun turret

11 cm (4.5 in) gun

F174

RADAR for gunnery and missile control

Stabilizer

Liferaft cylinder

Signal flag compartment

Reel

Fairlead

Anchor

Anti-submarine torpedo tube

Triple "chaff" rocket launcher

Bilge keel

Signal flag compartment

Pennant number

Porthole

SONAR bulge

Breakwater

Bollard

Draught (draft) mark

Fishing boats

FROM ITS ORIGINS THOUSANDS OF YEARS AGO, when nets were dragged by hand through the water or hooks hung from lines, fishing has developed into a great industry. By the late 19th century, fishing boats like the steam trawler shown here were ruthlessly efficient. Fleets of trawlers often served one factory ship which took the catch on board. Various types of net are used, including fixed traps, curtain-like drift nets, and funnel-shaped trawl nets. Nets can be laid at great speed with a netting needle. The catch is often gathered in baskets. Floats are arranged along the upper edge of a net to keep it buoyant. Modern technology makes tracing shoals of fish very easy. SONAR (SOund Navigation And Ranging) fish finders, for example, can even show the whereabouts of individual fish at the push of a button.

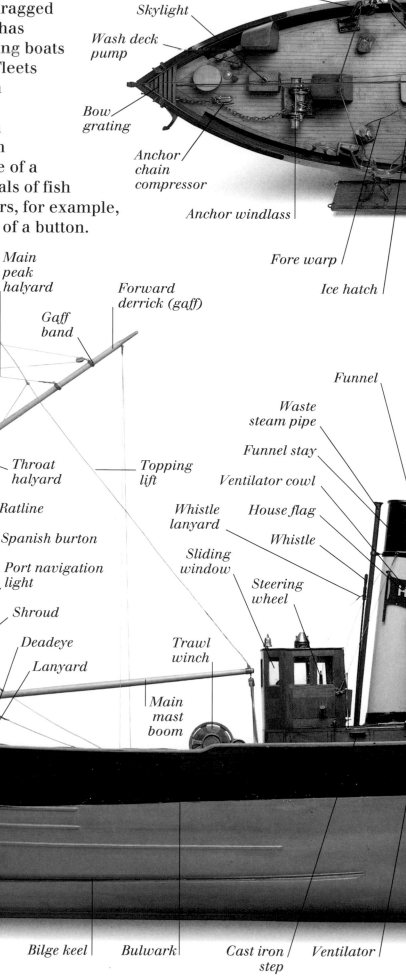

STEAM TRAWLER (DECK VIEW)

Fore gallows

Gallows bar

Skylight

Wash deck pump

Bow grating

Anchor chain compressor

Anchor windlass

Fore warp

Ice hatch

Tie

Handle

Randing

Willow stake

Woven base

Woven side

FISHING BASKET

Gilded truck

Main peak halyard

Steaming light

Topmast stay

Forward derrick (gaff)

Gaff band

Throat halyard

Topping lift

Funnel

Waste steam pipe

Funnel stay

Ventilator cowl

House flag

Whistle

Whistle lanyard

Sliding window

Steering wheel

Main mast

Ratline

Spanish burton

Port navigation light

Fore stay

Forward hanging block

Light screen

Shroud

Deadeye

Lanyard

Trawl winch

Main mast boom

Chimney scoot

Fo'c'sle stove chimney

Hawse pipe

Heads (privy)

Rodgers-type anchor

Fo'c'sle companion

Rubbing strake

Bilge keel

Bulwark

Cast iron step

Ventilator

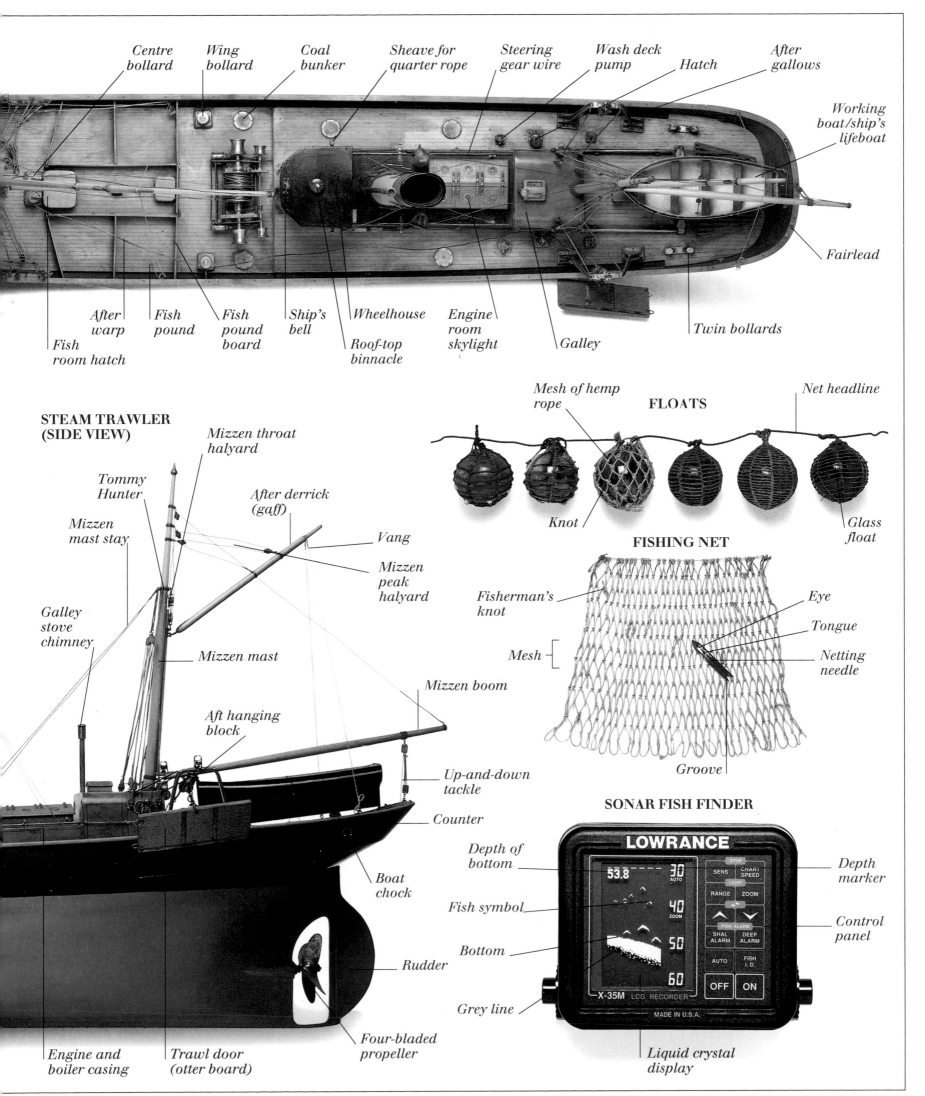

Centre bollard

Wing bollard

Coal bunker

Sheave for quarter rope

Steering gear wire

Wash deck pump

Hatch

After gallows

Working boat/ship's lifeboat

Fairlead

After warp

Fish pound

Fish pound board

Ship's bell

Wheelhouse

Engine room skylight

Twin bollards

Fish room hatch

Roof-top binnacle

Galley

STEAM TRAWLER (SIDE VIEW)

Mizzen throat halyard

Tommy Hunter

After derrick (gaff)

Vang

Mizzen mast stay

Mizzen peak halyard

Galley stove chimney

Mizzen mast

Mizzen boom

Aft hanging block

Up-and-down tackle

Counter

Boat chock

Rudder

Engine and boiler casing

Trawl door (otter board)

Four-bladed propeller

FLOATS

Mesh of hemp rope

Net headline

Knot

Glass float

FISHING NET

Fisherman's knot

Eye

Tongue

Mesh

Netting needle

Groove

SONAR FISH FINDER

Depth of bottom

Depth marker

Fish symbol

Control panel

Bottom

Grey line

Liquid crystal display

LOWRANCE

53.8

30 AUTO

STOP

SENS   CHART SPEED

LIGHT

40 ZOOM

RANGE   ZOOM

FISH ALARM

SHAL ALARM   DEEP ALARM

50

AUTO   FISH I.D.

60

OFF   ON

X-35M   LCG RECORDER

MADE IN U.S.A.

Under the sea

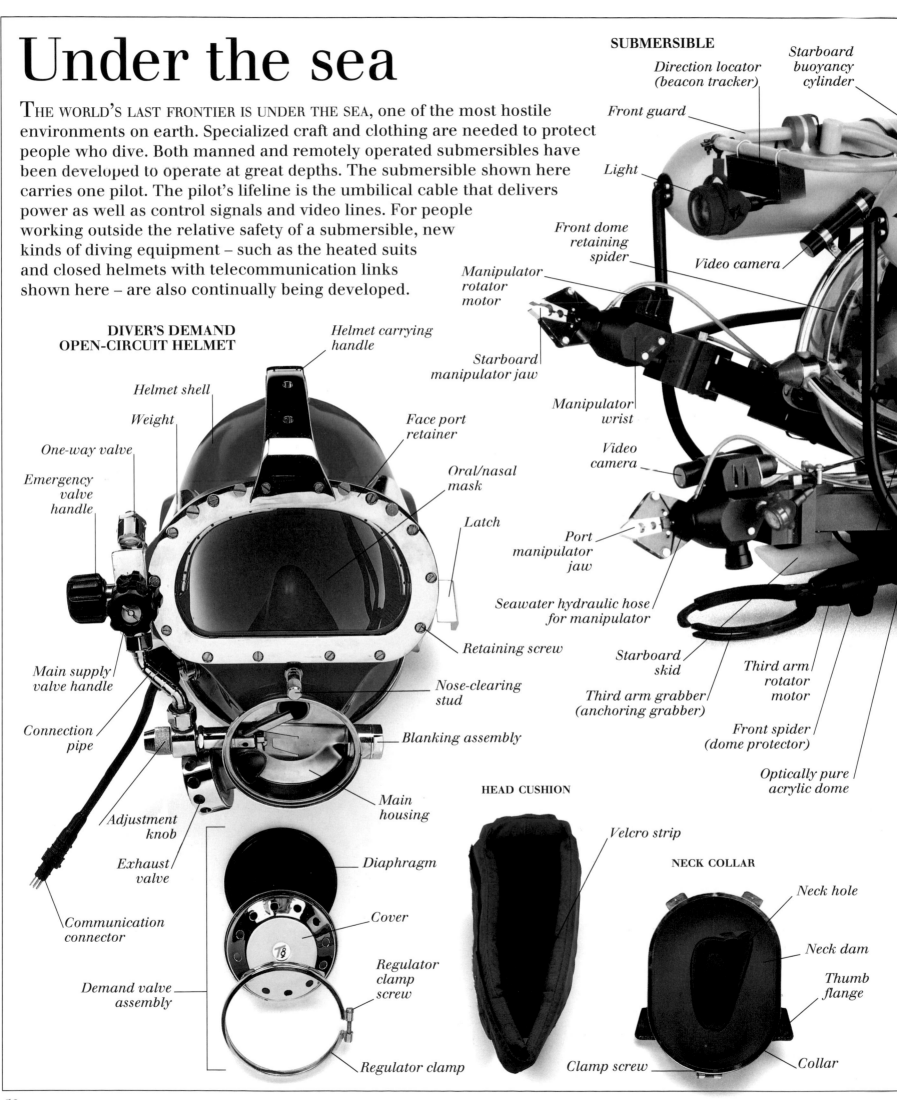

THE WORLD'S LAST FRONTIER IS UNDER THE SEA, one of the most hostile environments on earth. Specialized craft and clothing are needed to protect people who dive. Both manned and remotely operated submersibles have been developed to operate at great depths. The submersible shown here carries one pilot. The pilot's lifeline is the umbilical cable that delivers power as well as control signals and video lines. For people working outside the relative safety of a submersible, new kinds of diving equipment – such as the heated suits and closed helmets with telecommunication links shown here – are also continually being developed.

SUBMERSIBLE

Direction locator (beacon tracker)

Starboard buoyancy cylinder

Front guard

Light

Front dome retaining spider

Video camera

Manipulator rotator motor

Starboard manipulator jaw

Manipulator wrist

Video camera

Port manipulator jaw

Seawater hydraulic hose for manipulator

Starboard skid

Third arm grabber (anchoring grabber)

Third arm rotator motor

Front spider (dome protector)

Optically pure acrylic dome

DIVER'S DEMAND OPEN-CIRCUIT HELMET

Helmet carrying handle

Helmet shell

Weight

One-way valve

Emergency valve handle

Face port retainer

Oral/nasal mask

Latch

Main supply valve handle

Connection pipe

Retaining screw

Nose-clearing stud

Blanking assembly

Main housing

Adjustment knob

Exhaust valve

Communication connector

Diaphragm

Cover

Regulator clamp screw

Demand valve assembly

Regulator clamp

HEAD CUSHION

Velcro strip

NECK COLLAR

Neck hole

Neck dam

Thumb flange

Clamp screw

Collar

58

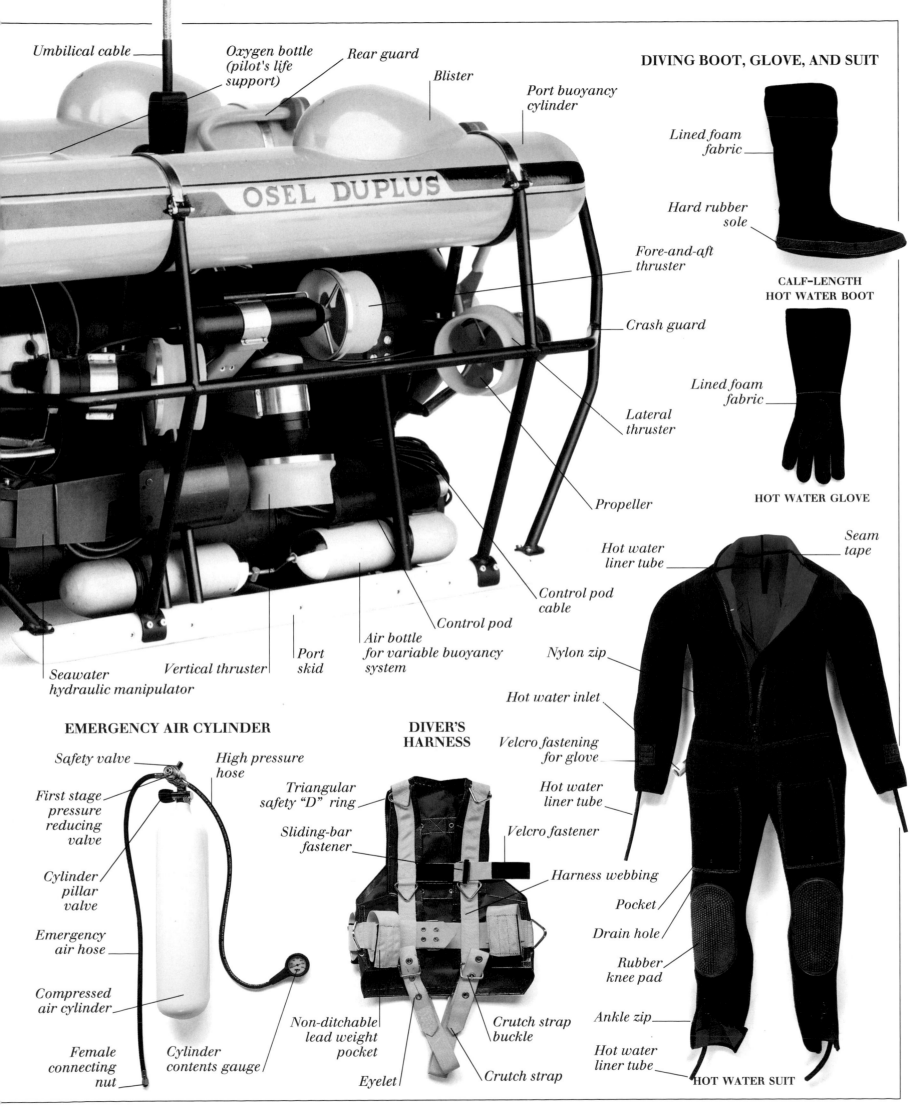

Umbilical cable

Oxygen bottle (pilot's life support)

Rear guard

Blister

Port buoyancy cylinder

OSEL DUPLUS

Fore-and-aft thruster

Crash guard

Lateral thruster

Propeller

Control pod cable

Control pod

Air bottle for variable buoyancy system

Vertical thruster

Port skid

Seawater hydraulic manipulator

DIVING BOOT, GLOVE, AND SUIT

Lined foam fabric

Hard rubber sole

CALF-LENGTH HOT WATER BOOT

Lined foam fabric

HOT WATER GLOVE

Hot water liner tube

Seam tape

Nylon zip

Hot water inlet

Velcro fastening for glove

Hot water liner tube

Velcro fastener

Harness webbing

Pocket

Drain hole

Rubber knee pad

Ankle zip

Hot water liner tube

HOT WATER SUIT

EMERGENCY AIR CYLINDER

Safety valve

High pressure hose

First stage pressure reducing valve

Cylinder pillar valve

Emergency air hose

Compressed air cylinder

Female connecting nut

Cylinder contents gauge

DIVER'S HARNESS

Triangular safety "D" ring

Sliding-bar fastener

Non-ditchable lead weight pocket

Eyelet

Crutch strap buckle

Crutch strap

59

Index

Acknowledgments

Dorling Kindersley would like to thank:
Geoff Hales and Harvey B. Loomis for advice; David Spence, Gillian Hutchinson, David Topliss, Simon Stephens, Robert Baldwin, Jonathan Betts, all of the National Maritime Museum, London; Ian Friel; Simon Turnage of Captain O.M. Watts of London Ltd., for sailing equipment; Davey and Company Ltd., Great Dunmow, for marine equipment; Avon Inflatables Ltd., Llanelli; Musto Ltd., Benfleet, for sailing clothing; Peter Martin of Spencer Rigging Ltd., Southampton; Peter Rowson of Ratseys Sailmakers, Southampton; Swiftech Ltd., Wallingford; Colin Scattergood of the Barrow Boat Company Ltd., Colchester; Tim Spalton of Glyn Locke (Racing Shells) Ltd., Chalgrove; Professor J.S. Morrison of the Trireme Trust, Cambridge; The Cutty Sark Maritime Trust; Adrian Daniels of Kelvin Hughes Marine Instruments, London; Arthur Credland of Hull City Council Museums and Art Galleries; The Hull Maritime Society; Gerald Clark for knots; Peter Fitzgerald of the Science Museum, London; Alec Michael of HMB Subwork Ltd., Great Yarmouth, and Ray Ward of the OSEL Group, Great Yarmouth, for access to submersible; Richard Bird of UWI, Weybridge, for diving equipment; Walker Marine Instruments, Birmingham; The International Sailing Craft Association; The Exeter Maritime Museum; Jane Wilson of the Trinity Lighthouse Company, London; The Imperial War Museum Collections; Daniel Bombigher; Thorn Security Ltd.; Michael Bach

Additional design assistance:
Nick Jackson, Johnny Pau

Additional editorial assistance:
Susan Bosanko, Deirdre Clark, Paul Docherty, David Harding, Edwina Johnson, Gail Lawther, Louise Tucker

Illustrators:
Roy Flooks, Linden Artists, John Woodcock

Model makers:
Richard Kemp, Kelvin Thatcher, Paul Wilkinson

Picture credits:
b=bottom, t=top, l=left, r=right
British Museum page 8bl; Michael Holford 10tr; National Maritime Museum 13br, 20-21b

The nautical chart on page 39 is Crown Copyright reproduced from Admiralty Charts/ Publications with the permission of the controller of Her Majesty's Stationery Office.

Picture research:
Clive Webster